SHAME

For those who have inspired me driven by courage and compassion, not self-interest or financial reward. For those whose reputations have been damaged because they were solely driven by a concern for the voiceless. For the selfless, who put aside their own needs and fears. For those who are prepared to change their views and listen to new evidence, challenge themselves and always examine what drives them each day. For those who put democracy, our freedom and our children first. This book is for you.

CONTENTS

The photo on the front cover was taken from inside BBC's New Broadcasting House during a protest in London on the 22nd January 2022. I have been told that it was passed around between staff at the BBC, but no one has yet come forward to claim ownership.

INTRODUCTION

No one wants to talk about lockdown. I understand that and I feel the same. But it must not stop me from publishing this book. I am in no doubt as a society we are suffering from a kind of collective post-traumatic stress disorder (PTSD) a symptom of which is avoiding any conversation that triggers a memory you want to forget. We all suffered - from the loss of loved ones, to the loss of our freedom. When you have PTSD, if someone mentions an incident or experience that was traumatic, you either leave the room, end the conversation, or try to change it. I can't even remember when lockdown started and ended, or how long the schools were closed. I can't remember the length of time or the dates. I know many people feel the same, experiencing poor memory with no desire to recall.

It has been enormously difficult to write this book and there is so much I have left out because every day I had a story to tell – and this period lasted for two years. The main horror for me, looking back, is what we did to our children. Closing the schools and playgrounds, forcing them to wear masks all day. On the bus and in all lessons apart from when they ate lunch or did P.E. I want to forget but, more than anything, I don't want this to ever happen again. In this book, I have tried to provide some answers, some solutions, but that really isn't its main purpose.

Together, we must one day have the courage to look back, to process and assess that period of our lives. I just wanted to record my story as I remember it. I started writing the book in 2021 and even then found it unbearable to record everything that was happening. That will be the first chapter you read. Then I continued writing in 2022 when it felt the horror was finally over. I am sorry if this is painful to read - I can assure you it was incredibly painful to write.

I thought so many more people would be brave, I thought they would stand up for what is right and decent. I thought they would listen to and protect the vulnerable in society. Were my expectations too high? If people didn't do the decent thing we suffer. We all suffer. We don't move forward collectively. We don't evolve. That is something I have just had to accept. That may be our future and it may be bleak. But if we are not driven by those important values - freedom, democracy and protecting our precious children - then we do not deserve to evolve. We will not evolve. And I am at peace with that.

WRITTEN IN JAN 2021

Today is January 5th 2021 and yesterday the UK Prime Minister, Boris Johnson, announced that England was to go into a second full lockdown, with schools shut until at least the February half-term. Wales and Scotland are to follow a similar policy.

In June 2020 I put together three videos; case studies from a children's counsellor.

These children's lives had been so badly impacted by the first lockdown but yet here we are again, nine months later. The big issue is trying to have faith and trust in a government and understand why hurting our children like this is necessary a second time around.

This is also the day that Talk Radio, one of the few media outlets challenging the Government's policy on lockdowns, had their *YouTube* channel taken down. I also lost mine on Christmas Day last year. It was the censorship and surveillance that concerned me most at the start of all of this and that feeling has not gone away.

Yes, I am feeling overwhelmed and rather numb. I had a lot of fight in me after the first lockdown, but how long can one maintain that same level of fight? My fight was for fairness. For all voices to be heard, especially doctors, professors, journalists, scientists, parents and others to be given a voice and for a healthy debate to be allowed that would make us all feel a lot less confused. It would build trust and make us feel comfortable that the decisions the Government were making were in our best interest. Without healthy debate and balance in the media, anxiety would only increase.

Yes, there is a virus that is killing people, in recent weeks there has been a surge in hospital admissions. Many hospitals in London are overwhelmed, treating people in the back of ambulances and possibly even turning people away. And if I had a family member who desperately needed treatment and was unable to get it, then I would agree tough action was needed. But I don't know if I would have wanted lockdown.

I have developed trauma over that word "lockdown", we are locked down - I didn't think it was possible that word would ever be used by a government, let alone enforced. But the UK Government felt it was the only option. Maybe it was, but I don't believe silencing those voices against a "lockdown", could ever be justified.

If you want to close the schools and make us stay in our homes, if you want to close the pubs, cinemas, gyms, swimming pools and churches, then please let us hear a healthy debate around why it was deemed necessary. Healthy debate has not been allowed and not only that, but some media organisations have gone out of their way to smear those who attempted to raise an alternative view. For example, look at the many articles from the *The Guardian* on the Great Barrington Declaration, which was authored by Dr Martin Kulldorff, who at the time was a Professor of Medicine at Harvard Medical School, Dr Sunetra Gupta, PhD, a Professor of Theoretical Epidemiology at Oxford University, and Jay Bhattacharya, MD, PhD, a Professor of Medicine at Stanford University Medical School.

I would also not have been able to comprehend back in March 2020 that we would still be here in January 2021. Everything is shut apart from essential food shops. We cannot meet with friends, we cannot go swimming, to the cinema, or to the gym. We can't do anything but sit in our houses and watch the cold winter sunshine light a world outside that still looks the same but isn't the same.

Society has been rocked to its very core; trust and faith in institutions such as the media and the Government has changed. I believe many people will never see them in the same way. Will we be for ever on edge, not sure if our leaders and our media brands are doing the right thing? Some people will feel their choices were the right ones, which is why I must reiterate that this is only my story in terms of how the media have handled the crisis. Here in the UK, it will take a very long time to heal from this trauma, where we can feel free to enjoy life as we used to.

If there is another virus, another strain, another public health emergency, we will be potentially waiting for the same extreme approach and a lack of debate around it. We will save more money than we used to due to fear of losing our jobs. We will be hesitant to enjoy too much of the things we used to take for granted, for fear that they may be removed again. I don't think I will ever be the same again. I had to put up an enormous fight to give people a voice and provide a much-needed counter narrative via my media channels. How much fight do I have to do that again? It is a mission that makes one weary and cynical. That visceral anger, shock and passion for justice has certainly diminished.

But I have met some wonderful people on this journey. I call them the compassionate and courageous. They have lost so much in terms of being smeared, mocked and losing professional credibility and, in some cases, their ability to make a living. Losing "income" does not sufficiently convey the human cost in my opinion. Many others have called them heroes. But have they made a difference? Have journalists/content creators, like me, just contributed to the chaos and confusion, where the rise of dissenting voices means a government can no longer control or organise its population?

Twenty years ago – even 10 years ago – we lived in a world where it was easy to manage the message. The social media platforms weren't as populated, our mobiles weren't as fast or as powerful, allowing us to communicate instantaneously with other people all around the world. I can do a zoom interview with a doctor in Canada, a professor in Germany and share to my thousands of followers, just as easily as I can interview the neighbour on my street. And it costs me nothing-bar a Zoom subscription.

Some people are not aware that BBC reporters are using their mobiles to film and edit TV news packages straight to broadcast on BBC1. Well, we can do the same and broadcast straight to *Facebook*, *YouTube* et al.

So, it all comes down to trust — who do you believe and who do you trust?

A public health emergency, combined with the power of global communication, was always going to lead us to this point. I felt it was coming.

I used to be a TV journalist and then, in 2017, I realised what I used to do was becoming more and more irrelevant. Everyone and anyone can be a TV journalist. Everyone can film, edit and publish with their mobiles. I trained corporate communications professionals to bypass the mainstream media via direct broadcasting. They can create their own professional content, rather than spending hours courting the old MSM (mainstream media) with press releases in a hope they would garner coverage.

So when this public health emergency came along and I felt important voices were being ignored, I simply used those skills of presenting, interviewing, filming and editing to build a platform where I could try and provide an important counter narrative I felt was missing, so all voices could be heard. I believed they needed to be heard and I felt it was essential that they were heard.

You cannot treat the public like children - that is an insult to children actually. They were treating the public like complete idiots. We all had access to *YouTube*, *Facebook* and *Twitter* and as soon as you see or hear something that goes against the Government narrative you can't unhear it. So if you can't unhear it and the Government or the old MSM media brands aren't covering it, you just feel panic and that something isn't right.

You stop trusting those you voted for - you feel the ground underneath you shake and a central, essential part of your life feels totally destabilised.

But I will tell you something - you go into battle and after so long you feel it is time to accept you have done what you can and it is time to walk away.

The trees, the fields, the animals, the birds, the sky all look the same but, as we look either at a screen or out of the window, we realise that is all we have. I was lucky because I had children to care for and love, but what about those people living on their own through this nightmare?

To save the hospitals from being overrun and being able to cope with the emergencies they must deal with, we have lost our freedom.

This is our new life and even Boris Johnson said last night there was no certainty that after the February half-term it will be over.

I try and remember what it was like to go to a comedy club, to the theatre, to call up a friend and go for coffee, wander around the shops, drink in a packed bar. I'm struggling to even remember what I used to do, or what I loved. I am depressed, I am numb but, more than anything, I am worried about the impact of this on our children.

So let's focus on the information we heard in 2020 that made us think or feel, or behave in a certain way. Why did we choose that information and where has it got us to now?

I had a relatively small *YouTube*, *Twitter* and *Facebook* following in March 2020, now I have about 70k followers on each platform. It grew because I felt no one was offering a counter narrative and, when professors such as Robert Endres from Imperial College London contacted me, I had to help.

When I saw the campaign group UsForThem needing help to raise awareness around how children were suffering during lockdown, I knew I could use my new media skills to assist. Film and edit on a mobile and broadcast at speed, in the same way I used to as a BBC and ITV reporter. Or do a strong and powerful interview with authority and publish on my *YouTube* channel. I knew I was as good as the breakfast TV presenters we saw every day; I had the look, the sound and I felt I could wake people up to the counter narrative - the voices we weren't allowed to hear.

To do this has taken its toll. I was a corporate communications media trainer in March 2020, then I became a personality but it was not something I felt comfortable with. But I had no choice, I had serious concerns about the future of our society. I wanted a balanced media that allowed debate and listened to all voices. I wanted a world where the police could not fine us for sitting on a bench or going for a walk. I wanted a democracy we could be proud of and trust in institutions such as health, education and the police. This is what would make my children feel safe. This is what had me feel safe up until March 2020.

My corporate clients soon fell away, one even emailed me to say - please remove our name from your website and do not ever mention again that you worked for us. I could have kept my views to myself like many did and moved my training on to Zoom. But how could I continue to market my mobile video workshops to corporate clients on LinkedIn? I couldn't. I saw too much suffering, I felt it was my duty to help. It would have felt obscene to not do something, no matter what the impact was to my income or business, or reputation. Some things simply matter more.

CHAPTER ONE - March 2022

That introduction was written in January 2021 and now it is March 2022. It is very interesting to read it, I thought at the time it was a just going to be a year that the world had gone mad. But now it transpires it was two years. In fact, the book was called "The Year The World Went Mad." If only.

The title of the book also needs to go with the image which was taken from inside BBC's New Broadcasting House in London, during a protest in London on the 22nd January 2022, more on this later, along with the contact I had with some BBC employees.

So, I come back to write again in 2022, with a new title and a new direction. And I start writing this book exactly two years after our first lockdown on the 23rd March 2020.

The main issue is how difficult it has been to absorb everything that has happened and to try and break it down and communicate it in a way that I hope future generations will really understand. There is no doubt about it, I am a different person, the experience changed me for ever.

I have been in touch with a publisher about the book. I put forward a submission and they very kindly responded after reading the first two chapters to say:

"Thanks for this. We've had a good editorial discussion about your proposal, but in the end, our concern is that because it's a review of what has happened, readers will have lost interest once this book is published, given the amount of media discussion these events have already had. But if you had an idea for another book, perhaps one that spoke to a future vision or idea, we would be very happy to consider."

A very polite reply, but one I simply could not understand. I think this must be seen as some kind of history book. It needs to be recorded as it happened. For us all to absorb and remember, as we all went through a very traumatic time. Our entire nation, every individual, was "locked down" effectively under house arrest and I certainly don't think the conversation has ended in relation to that.

Moving on and talking about something else is incredibly important, but we must record and reflect on what happened. Even if it is just to pass on to our children, so they can understand why their parents lost their jobs, or split up, changed careers, or drank too much alcohol. Why they missed two birthday parties, couldn't see their grandad or grandma, or go to the park. Our children will have memories of that period and will also want one day to understand.

As this book discusses the failings of established legacy media organisations, I should not be surprised that a mainstream publisher is not willing to take this on. They have established relationships of trust with the very media organisations I am about to criticise.

How the MSM, which I now call the old media, reported on the Covid crisis. We are all struggling to process memories and that collective experience is the most important moment in our history to date.

So, I know how we all have a memory and a story and an image that has stayed with us and I wish I could capture and reflect them all.

However, I do understand the power of an image and there were many.

For example, the image of Alyan Kurdi, the three-year-old Syrian boy from Kobane, washed up on a Turkish beach in 2015, had a huge impact on me. He was one of 12 Syrians who drowned off the coast of Turkey as they tried to reach the EU by boat. They were heading towards the Greek island of Kos.

A Turkish news agency shared the picture of his lifeless body being carried ashore by a Turkish policeman and it sparked a huge - and global - surge on social media.

Similarly, many photos and videos of that two-year Covid period are important and powerful and can evoke some of the feelings associated with that time for many of us.

I believe, like many people, I'm trying my very hardest to forget how bonkers our behaviour as a human species became. But remember we must because, if we don't, there is no doubt this collective insanity is at risk of returning.

I am sure we all need it to heal because it feels like it hasn't been processed. That now, in March 2022, we are focusing on inflation, sky-rocketing food and energy prices and the war between Russia and Ukraine. But I can sense people are dumbfounded, startled, confused, feeling that something weird just happened and are in denial, burying it even.

I'm trying my best to stay upbeat - and even laugh at how ludicrous it all was. Even though there was so much suffering, there were funny and bizarre moments.

I find we behave in one of three ways, or at least I do. You can get angry with others, angry with ourselves (and many started self-medicating with alcohol and drugs) or you laugh. What other options do you have? Harming others, harming yourself or laughing. And then finally - and this is what I want to focus on - how do we make sure our future looks like one that we can be excited about?

There is no shadow of a doubt my personal experience was traumatising. This house where I live is in the Vale of Glamorgan in Wales in the UK, under the stairs in my living room. This is where all of those Zoom interviews took place, first on my old Sony Vaio laptop, which really wasn't up to the job, then in early October 2020, just before my interview with former BBC presenter Sue Cook, I upgraded to a £350 HP laptop, thanks to my Patreon account which paid for it. And on this cheap laptop and a free zoom account, my interviews reached millions of people all around the world.

Here in my house under the stairs, interviewing Prof. Martin Kulldorff, Prof. Robert Endres, Dr Mike Yeadon, Dr Pierre Kory, Dr Tess Lawrie, Dr Roger Hodkinson, Dr Roland Salmon, Prof. Richard Ennos, along with MSM journalists, former senior news executives, politicians, taxi drivers, multi-millionaire businessmen and women. The founders of the main campaign groups in the early days - UsForThem, StandUpX, Save our Rights UK, Keep Britain Free, Stand in the Park. I worked hard and published as many interviews as I could.

When I met Christine Brett from UsForThem, and she told me she had been invited to speak on ITV's *This Morning* (May 2020) and then they dropped her at the last minute, I knew I had to do something. When Prof. Martin Kulldorff was mocked by the *Guardian* for speaking to a small alternative news channel, I knew I had to step in. When Prof. Richard Ennos told me a BBC reporter in Scotland admitted she was sent to smear him and other protestors and not listen to them; when BBC stalwart Sue Cook said she had turned off the BBC for the first time in 20 years, I knew I had to step in. When the BBC Trending disinformation/department went after Louise May Creffield, the brave and inspiring founder of Save Our Rights UK who was an integral part of organising those 2020 London protests, I knew I had to step in. What the hell were my former colleagues up to? What the hell was going on?

So there I was in lockdown on my laptop sitting under the stairs. And now this spot holds many memories for me - my anxiety levels are still raised sitting here with all the memories flooding back.

I will talk more about the people I met along the way, how they presented themselves to the old MSM and what their relationship was like with the new (alternative) media. I will discuss the important part the alternative media/social media had to play. How we managed to grow our voice and audience away from terrestrial TV news. You see, it wasn't just what Prof. Martin Kulldorff, for example, was saying, it was who he was saying it too.

I will also be talking about some of the journalists currently working for organisations such as Sky, the BBC and ITV, Guardian, The Mirror, The Express and others, including former colleagues I spoke to from my time at the BBC and ITV, but also new inspirational journalists I met along the way, who did their best to help.

There were many good guys trying their best, but they felt utterly lost. I was able to do the job they wanted to do. I have really pondered over this one, whether to name names, share secret recordings, private emails and phone recordings. Well, it is ethically and professionally seen as permittable should it be a matter of significant public interest - something so fundamentally important that it impacts many people.

So if BBC *Panorama* do secret filming in a care home - of residents being abused by staff for example - they would be able to publish that footage, despite the abusers not being aware that they were being recorded.

Alternatively, for example, Anne Robinson when she presented the BBC consumer programme *Watchdog*. They filmed trades people who perhaps told a pensioner her house needed a £2,000 rewire when it just needed a £120 quick fix. The BBC have guidelines for secret recording. We have seen the power of it in terms of sharing valuable information which the public would not ordinarily be privy to. But what are my rules in sharing these celebrities' and main TV news anchors' real thoughts and feelings during this incredible time?

Like the BBC's *Watchdog*, don't the same ethical principles apply here in terms of the BBC's rules on secret recording (which simply means publishing without their prior knowledge)?

If senior executives from news organisations such as ITV, Sky and BBC had contacted me and shared important information that was of huge public interest, am I professionally and ethically allowed to share that, providing I make them aware I am going to publish and offer them a right of reply? And should I share it?

What I would say is that these people had some power to change the narrative, they could have allowed a lot more debate. They could have alleviated a huge amount of suffering when it came to children, especially vulnerable children who were stuck at home during lockdown, not seeing their friends and family. The playgrounds were cordoned off, the schools shut. They were locked in their homes and I think of those living on a low income, with just one parent at home. They were the families I thought of. The ones who already suffered from anxiety, or perhaps were already experiencing some abuse or neglect at home. So how do I balance that with the conversations I had with people in the media, who knew very well the impact their actions/ publication had on these vulnerable children?

I got angry and, when I'd had a glass of wine, lost my temper with these MSM journalists and some senior TV executives. I wanted to know what the hell they were doing. But are these the people I should be turning on and exposing? Were these people the good guys only in the respect that they felt guilty and voiced it? They assured me that they were trying their best to change the narrative, to reform from within. But I really shouldn't call them the good guys, they were the best of a bad bunch. It was the journalists I used to work with who ignored me. They are the ones who I really am furious with. Some journalists who contacted me wanted to say thank you. They felt hopeless and helpless and they simply weren't in a powerful enough position to really make a difference.

We can easily become furious with these people who knew they were failing in their duty to allow debate, and hold power to account. To shame and smear brave professors such as the authors of the Great Barrington

Declaration, who were simply asking for a conversation around herd immunity. Those people who thought focused protection, shielding the vulnerable and elderly and allowing herd immunity in the young and healthy was a viable option. We must remember that this view was considered extreme and dangerous and it was the Government-funded narrative being pumped out on our TV screens and in the newspapers that sold us that ridiculous position.

Debate over lockdown was a form of heresy. Why? Because of appalling journalism. Their reporting over the last two years must remain a stain on their reputation for ever. I will continue to campaign for it to be labelled as the most profound and significant moment of shame the industry has ever felt and should ever feel again. We need to keep reminding them. And those journalists and executives who did feel uncomfortable - next time bloody well do something!

I know if I had still been at the BBC, I would have caused some serious trouble. I'd have worked out how to do it, to cause the maximum impact. Maybe saying something live on air, like journalist Ivory Hecker who announced live on air in June 2021 that she had been secretly recording her bosses at Fox 26 Houston. Or I would have worked out a secret code so I could connect with others who felt the way I did. In essence create a secret resistance movement from within, communicate through code, grow and go on strike and walk out. Why that didn't happen I don't know.

I did try and help people I knew at the BBC, but for whatever reason they couldn't find each other and organise themselves. But I couldn't betray their identity to each other. It was a very difficult situation and, looking back now, truly bonkers. I guess all we can really learn from this is to recognise what is important to us, what we really care about - and follow those core values and principles no matter what. So for me it's democracy, freedom and looking after our children. All of those things were massively under threat and still are to this day. Courage is a tough one. I know not everyone finds it easy. It is about doing the right thing and not even thinking about the consequences. You do it because you must do it, because it is the right thing to do.

But nothing - and I mean nothing stands in the way of me protecting my children, I would die for them in an instant. So–if I see my children and other children suffering, all other thoughts go out the window.

CHAPTER TWO - Looking Back

So, now let's go back to those images, videos and photos we all remember. What pops into my mind straight away is Holly and Phil from ITV's *This Morning* hugging through plastic sheets. A lot of people say to me that their first memory is the image from China of people collapsing in the street. Maybe it was the Italians singing opera to each other across balconies, when lockdown first hit Europe. Many of us felt we were watching a disaster unfold somewhere else, not here and never coming here. But, of course, it did.

Then we had the early images from the UK. Boris Johnson clapping for the NHS outside Downing Street while coughing with Covid. This was Thursday 2nd April 2020. Many of us may have forgotten that on the 6th April 2020 he ended up in intensive care for two days and at the time many of us considered the possibility that he might die.

We also had Donald Trump, the President of America at the time, testing positive for Covid on October 2nd 2020 and later that day he was transferred to Walter Reed

National Military Medical Centre to be released three days later. But as with Boris Johnson, again for a day or two the world thought he could die. When I mention these events, I think many people have forgotten about them, I know I had.

Here are some key stories and images as written up in some of our more established media brands that I remember:

29th March 2020, in the *Daily Mail*: "Black Day At Blue Lagoon." Picture shows a picturesque lake turned completely black after police put dye in it to "stop Instagrammers breaking virus lockdown". The background to this story is unclear and could probably make a whole chapter. A *Daily Mail* article from 2013 suggests that the police have been dyeing this lake every year to deter swimmers as the water is toxic. If this is the case, they should have been a lot clearer with their headline. But the point is people saw it and believed it and that must have added to the panic and confusion of the British public reading it at the time.

7th July 2020 *MailOnline*: "I don't want to die: Final interview with mother, 31, who died from bowel cancer leaves viewers absolutely devastated - after *Panorama* reveals her treatment was paused for six weeks during lockdown. Some two million screening tests for breast, bowel and cervical cancer have been missed, according to the show, sparking fears that thousands will face a delayed start to crucial treatment because of the pandemic."

5th October 2020 *The Express*: "Heartbreaking UK funeral video shows cruel moment an official forces son away from grieving mum. Fury as heartbreaking UK funeral video shows cruel moment upset mourners are torn apart."

5th November 2020 Sky News: "Coronavirus: Nurse arrested for trying to take mother with dementia out of a care home for lockdown."

26th February 2021 BBC News: "Wenatchee High School in Washington state wanted a way to allow students to rehearse safely during the pandemic. So they practiced in small green tents."

3rd April 2021 *The Guardian*: "Police break up Good Friday church service over apparent Covid rule breaches. Footage uploaded on *YouTube* showed Metropolitan Police officers addressing worshippers at the Christ the King Polish Catholic church in Balham south London, late on Friday afternoon."

I could go on and probably fill the book with them.

There were many horrific stories, but they didn't have a poignant image to go with them. But as I search back on my *Twitter* feed, this story from the 1st April 2020 pops up from the *Independent*: "A 13-year-old boy who died alone in hospital after testing positive for coronavirus is believed to be the UK's youngest victim of the pandemic. Ismail Mohamed Abdulwahab, who had no known underlying health problems, was admitted to King's College Hospital in London and put on a ventilator after having difficulties breathing. He died in the early hours of Monday without any family members present because of the risk of infection, according to a statement from the college where his sister works."

Those are the horrific stories for which we don't necessarily have a strong image or visual memory and I find those harder to remember. I have had to take some time out from writing after I read that article from the *Independent*. I am finding this very difficult to write about. I had forgotten or blocked out that we had left a 13-year-old boy to die alone in hospital.

....

And so to some other images. I know a lot were shared that were parody. I tried to avoid mentioning or ever sharing these myself as I could not verify if they were genuine. Remember the teens dancing back-to-back at a Covid prom. According to the insider.com this video was a joke and came from a dance school in the Czech Republic.

So many images that are most likely genuine could be parody. Like so much over the last two years, we lost our way in what was really happening and what wasn't. A lot of people just gave up on the MSM because they weren't allowing balance and debate, so they were living on a diet of *Telegram* and *Twitter*. Wasn't this the wild west where anything and everything gets shared? Parody and fantasy was certainly shared as if it were reality. A lot of people were turning to the *Telegraph*, with brave columnists such as Allison Pearson putting her head above the parapet pretty much from day one. Allison stood up, when everyone else was sitting down.

As bad as "some" of the legacy MSM have been, I know they had to adhere to journalistic standards or they'd be in trouble with the regulator. They would have to try their best to publish events and images that had actually happened. So I always felt safer sharing those, like the ones I have mentioned above.

The Good Friday service story, which was the lead in the *Mail Online* on the 3rd April 2021, was down to me. A follower sent it to me via email, as it was published on the church's *YouTube* channel. I passed it to the *Mail* and it was their lead story by the end of the day. I didn't get paid for this, I didn't care about being paid, I just wanted this horror to be shared with the public, they had a right to know. It was reported by the BBC News website on the 3rd April 2021: "A Good Friday service at a Catholic church in south London was shut down for breaching national lockdown restrictions, police said.

Met Police said officers found some worshippers without masks and not socially distancing at Christ the King church on Balham High Road on Friday.

Video of officers addressing the congregation, from the altar of the church, has been circulating online."

The issue of what is true and what is not, what is fake and what is real has never been more important and I knew immediately we were in trouble.

I have had a very close relationship with many people in what I would call the truther movement (another term you might use is conspiracy theorist) and their ability and trust to see what is real and what is not has been really damaged, as has mine. But who can blame them? We are all feeling lost. Bruised, bewildered and craving some control over our future, should this nightmare ever happen again. We need to know where to go and who can lead. This was a total cock up let's face it, and the hope of this book is to make sure we learn from our mistakes.

CHAPTER THREE - Politics

It's now May 2022 and it is confirmed that Boris Johnson and his government broke lockdown rules on multiple occasions. From a cheese and wine party in May 2020, to an unauthorised gathering at the Conservative party HQ on 14th December 2020. The following day there was a Christmas quiz for No10 staff and then many leaving parties are believed to have taken place on the 16, 17, 18 December 2020 and the 14 January 2021 and 16 April 2021.

What I would say is, in trying to bring a little bit of hope and optimism to this book, there are two years until the next general election. What a fabulous opportunity for new political parties to grow very fast from the amazing grassroots organisations we have here in the UK, such as Stand in the Park, Save our Rights UK, or the children's group UsForThem and the Together declaration.

In December 2021, the Liberal Democrats won the North Shropshire by-election taking a seat the Tories had held for almost 200 years. Helen Morgan won by nearly 6000 votes, overturning a Conservative majority of almost 23,000. And how did they do it? With a very powerful image from lockdown: On one side Boris "partying" and the other an elderly lady stuck at home not allowed to go out. It wasn't difficult. As soon as I saw it, I knew the LibDems would win. They used an image - a simple image sent to every home in the constituency. Powerful words and an image that voters would connect with.

If nothing else comes of this book, I hope it inspires the grassroots movements to seriously consider putting forward an independent candidate, or their own candidates, in the next general election. Let's look at long-term goals and aims. Now would be the time for them to start campaigning, building relationships with their local media and with the public.

Building trust and establishing fresh political or media brands takes time, but it is certainly achievable especially using social media. *Facebook* in particular is a very powerful tool for people needing to build a brand locally and establishing themselves as something new and fresh for the future. It works beautifully on a local level, especially if you have a budget for geotargeted boosts. It is something I have done very successfully with my two local news brands Penarth and Barry SMTV.

Rather than complaining about our democratically elected leaders, why don't we replace them?

I have seen many politicians producing short news videos on their mobiles to share on social media, people such as Conservative MP for Wycombe Steve Baker. They are the brand, they are the news and they get it straight out on *Twitter* or *Facebook* via direct broadcasting. Steve regularly shares images from tours around his constituency, talking to local artists, visiting museums, planting trees and attending events. He seems to be listening to his community and doing some great local news. He doesn't need to hang around ITV Central News, which MP Keith Vaz did when I was there in 2004 (old school publicity for old school politicians). He has a mobile and he has a platform. It's called direct broadcasting and it works.

As with politics, new media brands can do something similar but, so far, they are not all growing or being taken seriously.

But a word of caution. The brave, wonderful, caring people who fought hard during lockdown in my opinion, appear to be in limbo. Many think the lockdowns and vaccine mandates could come back this winter but there is no indication of this. I am distancing and detaching myself from people who have a cynical view of the future and seem to be on constant tenterhooks. It appears to be over guys, let's have a party -enjoy our freedom and move on. Learn from our mistakes and make sure it never happens again. Possibly ridiculously naïve but let me have my moment to smile and rest. Maybe my mental health needs this, and maybe I am horrifically wrong with this prediction, but I will discuss this in detail later in the book.

I am not saying that we do not need to be on guard in terms of future potential threats to our freedom, such as discussions on how the World Health Organisation (WHO) might manage future pandemics.

In February 2022, negotiations took place on new rules for dealing with pandemics with a target date of May 2024 for a treaty to be adopted by the UN health agency's 194 member countries. It is important we keep abreast of these developments. Is the WHO trying to take over the decisions individual countries were able to make in 2020? A global organisation we didn't vote for having that kind of power, I am sure makes us all feel a little queasy.

But there is still much to look forward to. There is no doubt many are still focused on the past, still in stunned disbelief that any of that just took place, others are meeting up socially like Stand in the Park groups. Some are taking time out and having a break and others are getting ready for the next general election. I had an attendee at one of my mobile video workshops looking to build her presence on social media as she prepared to stand in Dorset in the next election.

This for me seems a very positive and useful way to:

1. Have a real say in our future.

2. Ensure that nonsense never happens again.

3. Discuss the issues which are broader now. After lockdown many of our town centres and communities don't look the same.

26th Feb 2022 *DorsetLive*, Kate Maclachlan writes: "We counted the number of empty shops in Bournemouth town centre following high-profile store closures. High streets throughout the country have suffered in recent years as shops move online and the pandemic lockdowns forced people to stay local. However, some have seen a particularly high decline in shops with many shopfronts remaining empty for years. They list the 35 empty shop fronts taken from the retail areas of Commercial Road, Old Christchurch Road, Old Christchurch Road, The Triangle and Post Office Road. Many closed during lockdown and never re-opened."

This is good local journalism and needs to be talked about. Our new independent politicians or those from new political parties can focus on these important community issues.

In my home town of Newent in Gloucestershire, there have been significant changes following lockdown. It has a population of just over 5,000 people and, while new houses are going up at a pace I have never seen before, amenities are going the other way. The world-renowned Birds of Prey Centre has closed, a well-known Christian book shop and coffee shop has closed, a large pub and restaurant has gone the same way, all of the banks have shut and bus services have stopped to Ross-on-wye and Ledbury. These are services and businesses that had been established for more than 30 years.

My mum, who is 75, has lived in Newent nearly all of her life and is distressed and shocked to see the town she loves change beyond recognition. Are these businesses no longer economically viable following a change in our lifestyle and habits during lockdown? Are we now so used to online shopping never to return to the High Street in large numbers? The Government stopped us from socialising, we got used to watching Netflix, working from home and conducting life through our laptops and mobiles.

This is a focus for all of us, a hope and vision for the future -let's build back our communities. That makes me the antithesis of Maggie Thatcher. She said in 1987 in an interview in *Woman's Own*:

"They are casting their problems at society. And, you know, there's no such thing as society. There are individual men and women and there are families. And no government can do anything except through people, people must look after themselves first."

Are we losing our communities? Has Maggie's vision already come true? Are we scared to be vulnerable, to be close with each other and talk about the impact the last two years have had on our lives?

Many of us, understandably, are avoiding conversations about the last two years, we are packaging it into a memory, like a horrible dream that we have now awoken from that must be quickly forgotten. That was then, this is now and please let's not talk about it. People died from lockdown and people died from Covid and we all went through a very strange and difficult time and it is best to just forget it all now as a bad dream. But I often think about how my children saw the pandemic and what they would want to happen now.

Maybe I just want my children to read this book more than anything and understand why their mum appeared to go a little crazy. And perhaps one day they will be proud of me.

And I don't want to judge people. Decent people who I thought would behave in a good and honourable way didn't. But that was their choice and that was all I was ever really fighting for - choice - and they made a choice. So It is not for me to judge, or expose or criticise people for the choices they made in that moment.

CHAPTER FOUR - Strength to Remember

As I delve into my memories and my tweets, *Facebook* and *YouTube* posts going all the way back to 2020, I expect like me you will go aha, yes of course, I remember that now. I remember how I felt then. I think more than anything I connected with people emotionally and when I did my interviews and pieces to camera, I was very emotional. That is just the way I am. I tried to read as many comments across my channels as I could and absorb what people were saying and to reflect on that in my work. Reflect on how they were feeling, and how I was feeling and put that across to the public.

So, let's start from March 2020 as that is where it all kicked off for all of us.

In March 2020 I had a full diary of work doing my two-day mobile video workshop with bookings from the Professional Golf Association, a communications team in Aberdeen (flight booked), Wales and West Utilities and numerous others. My work came in via word of mouth and I was at the stage where I was putting up my prices and turning clients away due to a full diary. I could not believe how much fun I found the training. I would work mainly with corporate communications teams. The work was well paid and really enjoyable. I did a freelance reporting shift at ITV Central in Birmingham where I was paid £170, but it took two hours to get there from where I live near Cardiff to the ITV offices in Birmingham, and, with my costs of travel and staying overnight, being a regional reporter wasn't going to work for me. In addition, their content was becoming more and more irrelevant as the public were sharing far more local stories, in real time via *Facebook* and other social media platforms. I was also earning a lot more with my new training business. Life was good.

But then the shock announcement of lockdown came. My children were all at primary school at the time. Some pupils at this school, who had parents from European countries such as Germany, Italy and Finland, were taking their children out before the lockdown announcement.

I remember each day on the run up to the 23rd March 2020 seeing fewer and fewer parents on the school run and my children told me that, while class numbers had been high on the Monday, by the Friday before lockdown they halved each day. A class of 25 went down to eight by the end of the week.

It all felt incredibly surreal, there was no point of reference for me in terms of a memory or experience that had matched it in the past. I remember walking to school and filming it, as it was incomprehensible to me, just a bizarre, strange time. This was the start of me wanting to catalogue the period, I knew it needed to be captured.

That first week, a good friend of mine snapped at me, suggesting I should also take my children out of school before any planned announcement regarding full school closure. She was not the type to snap and I was shocked. She believed that a killer virus was on its way and we needed to act fast. I could see her fear had turned to panic and I knew the BBC and ITV, my former employers, had a part to play.

The 23rd March 2020 was a Monday - and we all sort of knew it was coming. Lockdowns were being announced all over Europe. I think I had this naive hope that it wouldn't happen, I thought it was so ridiculously extreme and I couldn't really understand why it was necessary.

So with the children not in school and all work cancelled, I was just in a state of shock. What was there to do other than go to the supermarket, drink alcohol and watch TV? Going for a walk even seemed to cause problems back then too.

And the other thing I started to do was record videos on my mobile, the pieces to camera a lot of people remember, saying what a lot of people were thinking at the time. I felt it was important to keep a video diary of what was happening as it was all unprecedented. I felt compelled to keep a record of the unfolding phenomenon.

And this is how it all kicked off:

My very first video on *YouTube* was about the Californian doctors being censored. Do you remember them? The two doctors sitting in navy tunics who held a press conference in April 2020. Dan Erickson and Artin Massihi presented their medical advice in a video during a press conference. It went viral, gathering more than 5.46million views before *YouTube* took it down.

That was the first video I remember doing and my sleepy *YouTube* channel was suddenly alive with 84k views.

My focus at this moment in time was that two doctors had been removed from *YouTube*. I had never in my entire life witnessed such censorship and I found it deeply shocking. I'd started a *YouTube* channel in 2015 but it had never really taken off. My content focused on media training and mobile journalism. My showreel from my time at ITV and the BBC was on there and a 10-minute local news programme I had produced using my mobile.

But then I used that same *YouTube* channel to publish these short pieces to camera, simply sharing my thoughts, feelings and observations of some of the stories we were hearing at the time. And it quickly gained traction, from many people in the media and from the general public. I'd create short two to three-minute videos, and publish to my *Facebook*, *Twitter* and *YouTube* channels. And I found very quickly that a lot of people were thinking and feeling the same way as me and all the channels grew very quickly.

I tried my hardest to provide calm and fair commentary, balancing the risk that the virus posed, with the risk and suffering people were experiencing being stuck at home.

Lots of influencers and celebrities started saying the same thing and we soon started connecting, including on a WhatsApp group that grew rapidly with hundreds of members before it was closed down on the 25th February 2022. We were horrified quite frankly, panicking and in shock and finding each other for support and for ideas on what we could do. Some very big names in terms of celebrity status were on this group, but they only stayed a month or two. And I can guess what happened; their celebrity agents told them to protect their reputation and privacy regarding opinions on this sensitive issue. This was later confirmed by people who I connected with.

The advice I am sure would have been to say nothing, keep your thoughts to yourself, as the herd immunity and lockdown argument was just not one that was allowed to take place at the time. Remember, back then there was no talk of mandating masks and the vaccine had not been developed. It was all about herd immunity and lockdown and, as I said, you weren't allowed to discuss the merits of herd immunity. It was framed as a reckless and dangerous option that meant you advocated an unacceptable risk that meant thousands of people could die.

I don't need to say who these celebrities and influencers are, I hope they tell their own stories one day. But for me to observe their behaviour was fascinating. I could see they had to split themselves, their personal and private opinions in direct opposition to what they were saying publicly. They had such passion and anger around the lack of debate between herd immunity and lockdown, but the advice from their agents would be to just stay quiet.

I can't live that way, especially when it comes to children suffering. I have to speak up, no matter what the cost. In my mind, I saw a single parent with five children and no family support struggling in a flat, with no garden, no school, and absolutely nowhere to take the children. I knew vulnerable children were immediately being put at risk. Parents were already struggling and feeling trapped.

But I was also aware that, for many, lockdown was fantastic, a long holiday with their children and partner and time to enjoy walks out and time at home. I knew many people and I understood that these two very different and opposing experiences were our reality.

On a visit to Morrisons supermarket in Barry, South Wales during the first few weeks of lockdown, I saw an older gentleman walking around the store chatting to people. The woman on the checkout said he was in there every day for hours, as his church had closed. He lived on his own and wanted to connect with people. She said he was putting his life at risk and may catch Covid. I felt his loneliness and I was upset that he could no longer socialise.

In January 2022 the UK looked very different to countries such as Italy, where vaccinated children were still in masks and will be up until term ends in June 2022. I know about Italy, thanks to a very honest friend who I worked with at ITV in Birmingham. She could not understand the lack of balances and checks in relation to Covid and felt masks and vaccine passports made her and her family feel safe. But she was honest with me about the real situation they faced in Italy and still do up to this day in 2022. I thank those who did speak to me candidly and helped me to reflect what was happening around Europe and the rest of the world.

I was also in contact with people in Ireland, where the unvaccinated were not allowed to enter cafes, restaurants gyms etc, without a vaccine passport. One Dublin-based resident I spoke to said her dog ran into the restaurant and was allowed in, but she wasn't.

This didn't really happen in the UK. So people did speak out—and yes, they did make a difference, I think. The resistance was strong from day one. And we had what a contact called 'elite dissent', in terms of the *Telegraph* and the *Spectator* sharing good articles on important issues around herd immunity and the merits of lockdown.

Many people were brave in speaking out from day one and I think that set us on the right path. This book would take me forever to write if I mentioned them all. There are, of course, people who immediately stand out to me and what has upset me quite a lot is that we haven't said thank you or had a big party. I understand the immense pressure they were under, the sacrifices they made to help the UK look like it does now. To fight lockdowns and vaccine mandates. That was the horror we were all battling. We were fighting for the right to choose. I will always stand with people who were brave enough to debate a narrative that allowed us to choose.

Now in May 2022, I often see people wearing masks, maybe two per cent of the population and I feel really happy as I know it is their choice and it is my choice not to. They have looked at the evidence and made their own health choices based on what they have read and seen.

That is the world I thought I lived in before March 2020. I often think to myself about how the Government could have sold lockdown to me, so that I would have happily accepted it. The answer is that if at least 10-20 per cent of the population was dying.

I know the risk and fear was that the hospitals would be overwhelmed, and people would not be able to receive treatment. But the Government could have made that very clear and then said, bearing in mind that is the risk, stay open and go about your daily business as you wish, but that you may not be able to get hospital treatment if you get ill.

That seems fair to me. But I can appreciate that to some this would appear brutal and extreme. Also, I guess the question would be, how would you prioritise patients? It was a tricky one and not an easy decision for any Government I am sure.

But then my feelings sharply changed and I became clearer on the type of information I felt the public should be hearing and were not.

Prof. Robert Endres got in touch from Imperial College London—and the subject of herd immunity was introduced by the Great Barrington Declaration in October 2020. At this point, there was a very clear need for debate and challenge over lockdown policy. And that simply didn't happen.

From May 2020 onwards we started to hear from professors such as Sunetra Gupta from the University of Oxford, about the possibility of bringing in a herd-immunity strategy or focused protection, one whereby the vulnerable and elderly were shielded at home, and the young and healthy were back out in society, living again and catching Covid and building up herd immunity.

I paid very close attention to how Prof. Sunetra Gupta was viewed by media brands and channels such as the BBC and *Twitter*. She was on a variety of news programmes, including the BBC, but she was always a minority voice and one that horrified many. It was not a 50:50 debate between her and other voices.

We must never forget that we were simply not allowed to talk about focused protection or herd immunity. We were effectively all under house arrest and attempting to even question whether that was right or not was putting us at risk of unpleasant and vile comments from others. One narrative dominated our lives and no conversation, dissent or debate was allowed around it.

But us influencers with social media platforms *were* talking about it, and that came with a lot of risk and abuse. The Great Barrington Declaration was not launched until October 2020. I remember Freddie Sayers from *UnHerd* involved in the launch speaking to Professor's Martin Kulldorff, Sunetra Gupta and Jay Bhattacharya from the universities of Harvard, Oxford and Stanford.

Of all the journalists I watched during that time, Freddie Sayers for me was the most inspirational because he kept his cool. Unlike me, he did a good job to take his opinion out of it; he kept calm and he brought in balance. He exuded credibility and authority and that really helped people like myself, and other influencers discuss these important issues without being smeared and laughed at.

He was in the space I wanted to be, but my emotions overwhelmed me. And I am not very good at hiding that. When I could see people suffering, it was very hard for me to stay clam. There were many other journalists who inspired me, but I have to say Freddie stood out above the rest at this particular time.

I also started chatting to Christine Brett, one of the original founders of UsForThem, the group focusing on the harms of lockdown and masks on children. I will never forget my horror as she told me her daughter was expected to wear a mask on the school bus. Then within six months, this became accepted as the norm.

I also travelled to London to meet wealthy businessman and entrepreneur Simon Dolan who founded Keep Britain Free, where I also met Leah Butler Smith who helped to organised the very first protest, which at the time was covered by Sky News.

Simon was one of the few who spoke out from day one. He was able to raise nearly half a million pounds to fund a judicial review. What I found fascinating is how Sky News did cover this very first protest in July 2020 in a calm and balanced way despite there only being about 100 people there.

As we know, later protests mainly organised by Save Our Rights UK were not covered in the same way. They were either completely ignored by the British media or the protestors were called names, like conspiracy theorists and anti-vaxxers when many simply just wanted their freedom of choice back. What was interesting from my perspective at least is that I felt in those early days Simon and Leah were listened to by the likes of Sky News and ITV's *This Morning*.

I knew Simon Dolan was on the Sunday Times Rich list in 2020 and reported to be worth £200 million. He was a partner at a PR company called the PHA group. I could see how this had an impact on how the Keep Britain Free and judicial review campaign was reflected in the media. Money of course buys you favourable headlines and coverage.

Back then I also tried to find out more about StandupX who were very vocal on social media at the time. I believe Piers Corybn was involved with this group and they were more outspoken and I believe very quickly lost their *Facebook* pages and groups. And finally Louise May Creffield who set up Save our Rights UK. They still have a very strong presence and a large following on social media.

That very first meeting with Simon Dolan and Leah at a five-star hotel in central London was very interesting. Sitting there having afternoon tea I wondered for what other reason three strangers would have been brought together like this. But we discussed Louise from Save Our Rights UK and Simon said he'd had meetings with her and the others leading the early resistance movement. He explained that we needed some kind of hierarchy and that someone needed to be in charge. But he explained that Louise had argued that should not be him, just because he was wealthy. She had a point, but right from day one we tried to organise ourselves.

These people were fab, Simon was kind and generous, as was Louise. I found them to be passionate, brave and caring people and over the next two years I met many more like them.

The one thing I would say is that there were so many organisations, ranging from those campaigning for our rights and freedoms to be restored, children-focused campaigns, protest groups, doctors' groups and then later groups of MSM journalists and celebrities. I tried my best to keep up with them all and help where I could. Apart from Simon Dolan, Keep Britain Free and one or two appearances for Christine

Brett and the team from UsForThem, they weren't being heard by the media organisations I used to work for. I felt they needed to be heard – there was so much energy behind these campaigns – caring, professional people who wanted to be part of the debate. I could do my bit in getting their voices heard and I tried to do my best.

We were all able to connect via social media, particularly *Twitter*. I remember communications consultant James Melville, who has a very large following on *Twitter*, was one of the first to speak out against lockdown and was criticised by Peter Jukes, co-founder and executive editor of *Byline Times*. I believe James had done some work with him in the past and were on good terms but, due to differing views on lockdown, they fell out quite publicly on *Twitter*. Peter Jukes also went for me and others, so it was then easy for us to find each other. We formed our own communication group and it quickly grew.

In September 2020, I saw a tweet from Mike Wendling, who was the Editor of BBC Trending at the time and managed journalists like reporter Marianna Spring. He implied that no one at the BBC remembered me. It was spiteful, personal and unprofessional. I followed up with a direct message asking him to correct what he said and to contact my former bosses at the BBC in Southampton and Cardiff who would confirm what I did and when I was there. I made some good friends at the BBC and enjoyed working there and got on well with everyone. He didn't like that and I don't believe I ever got the correction. I believe he has now deleted that tweet, but I still have a record of the direct messages.

But looking back, I suppose these people like BBC's Mike Wendling, Marianna Spring did us all a favour and the likes of Dom Joly, Peter Jukes and Piers Morgan. They enabled us to connect with others who had also been publicly smeared and laughed at for asking important questions and calling for debate around the draconian lockdown measures enforced on us all. This and my own broadcasts and publications led to me having direct contact with a number of high-profile celebrities and influencers. It was the most unbelievable and bizarre period of my life and I am sure nothing in the future will compare.

Some of these high-profile individuals are household names, presenting the most popular TV programmes we watch every day. Some said publicly what they could, although this was a very diluted and managed message in the odd tweet here or there. I have no doubt some were warned by their agents to 'SHUT UP and SHUT UP FAST or you will never work again'. One celebrity told me that their agent said they needed to take out a full-page apology in one of the national papers or they would never work again. It appeared to be the agents–that were taming these brave, fiery celebrities.

The message was simple: If you don't shut up, you will never work again. This is career suicide.

But we know who ignored this advice and we must take the time to thank them now in 2022. These people are our future and we must celebrate whatever incredible spark and sacrifice that is within those people who thought, 'f*ck it'. I always call them the courageous and compassionate. And let's be honest, it certainly wasn't just celebrities. It was teachers, doctors, solicitors, barristers, journalists, professors, nurses, taxi drivers, shop workers, the list goes on. I know while I write this, all of you have different names popping in into your head. I stood with these guys, I proudly stood with these guys. We MUST celebrate and discuss their bravery as this energy, this spirit, whatever you want to call it, must not die.

And I do worry should anything like this happen again that we are all war weary and compassion fatigue has set in. It certainly has with me. And these guys may be thinking, 'I did my bit, been there done that and look where it got me. Will I do it again? Has it been worth it?' People such as Matt Le Tissier, who has said in recent interviews that he lost his job as a contributor on Sky Sports because of his opinions on the Government's response to Covid. He has been picked on, attacked and smeared, subjected to a concerted campaign to basically ruin his reputation. All he did was question lockdown, and he lost his job. I asked Alistair Bunkall, who is now the Middle East correspondent for Sky News, whether he wanted to work for an organisation which did this. He and I worked together briefly at ITV Central in Oxford. He didn't reply. But I do appreciate that he entered into many conversations and did debate with me over lockdown, mask and mandated-vaccinations for children.

But in terms of Matt Le Tissier, will he bother to speak up should this happen again? Is the reward knowing he stood up for choice, for freedom, for our future, enough for him? Well, I hope so.

I must have had two or three messages a day, via email or *Twitter*, saying that I was keeping people sane. That I must not stop, that I am their hero. Wow, that was nice. And so many people approach me now in 2022 saying I kept them sane. It didn't pay the bills, but let's be honest, we all love to hear that.

I think part of me did feel like some kind of wonder woman. It all felt like a complete and utter bizarre, crazy dream. I was chatting with celebrities that I would never have spoken to in a million years if it wasn't for my profile and following on social media.

I respected their wishes to keep their thoughts private, but there was one I did get very angry with, a main TV news anchor. It was when it became clear the Government were going to start vaccinating children and I knew this person could do something and I lost it. I made a veiled threat to expose them.

I regret this, but at the time I was balancing these two decisions in my mind. These people who spoke to me were the best of a bad bunch. They were the ones talking about this insanity, why would I expose them for trying to help? If they wanted to speak out, that was their choice to make.

I feel a lot calmer now about the issue of vaccinating children against Covid, because it is a choice. People seem pretty chilled out about that now where I live. It was the mandating of anything that disturbed me. If parents want to take a risk on the vaccine, then fine, go ahead. They might also want to feed their kids aspartame diet drinks every day, and suck on a bag of boiled sweets continually and never take them to the dentist, or let them stay up until 1am every night watching inappropriate crap on TikTok. Each to their own is how I feel now.

Parents have been making horrific decisions in terms of their children's health for centuries and it is not for me to judge that or get involved. The problem I have is peer pressure and mandation. Our health choices should be private and down to us to make without sharing with others.

But I do feel we need to pat ourselves on the back here in the UK, as I have not really sensed that happening too much when it comes to children. It feels like we have been given the freedom to choose when it comes to their health. The situation is completely different in many other parts of the world.

So in terms of those brave, caring people who did speak up: thank you guys, even if I can't name you all. We all did our bit. I can think of so many people who have inspired me, who supported me and who I will for ever owe a debt of gratitude.

When the time came for us to be brave and fight we did it. Will we do it again if we need to? I have no idea.

CHAPTER FIVE - The Celebs

So let's briefly talk about celebrities, from the A listers to the Z listers. To me they were all the same. Some took bigger risks in sharing their true feelings, others were less brave. They can look back now and reflect whether or not they are happy with that. What we were all hoping for was a very high-profile celebrity saying high-stake things, but I'm not sure that ever really happened.

I am not into the whole celebrity thing and when people act all weird around me, I hate it. Once someone in the local shop saw me and they looked like they started to shake. There are two celebrities I can think of now who are big-name TV presenters for the MSM and they acted as if *I* were a celebrity. "They went oh my God it's you! Thank you, thank you. You are amazing."

Chatting to some of these people on the phone or over WhatsApp was weird, but reverence was given to those with a bigger profile, and probably more to lose in terms of reputation and I didn't like that as I think we should speak about everyone equally.

The only celebs I really respected were the ones taking genuine risks. Tiptoeing around the luvvies and making them feel appreciated and adored for daring to reveal a tiny glimpse of how they were truly feeling and the impact it was having on their luvvie lifestyles wasn't really my cup of tea.

After a few months many of them left the WhatsApp group I mention. That was probably wise, as new people were joining and they couldn't manage what was said or how that could be leaked. Wise, in terms of protecting their career and income, their reputation. We have seen how quickly these can get destroyed by legacy MSM brands.

It was exciting to be hearing the real thoughts and feelings of these people who I would never have had anything to do with, if it weren't for Covid. But I'd been there and done it in terms of wanting to be famous and it was out of my system. I'd worked on my ego and realised I had only gone into TV because I was badly bullied at school and needed it to boost my self-esteem. After taking a two-year counselling course and having therapy myself, I knew deep down that I was a quiet private person and that the new media training career I had suited me a lot better.

Working in ITV and BBC regional newsrooms there were a lot of characters who were a bit like Alan Partridge. Harmless individuals who I could see adored the one or two pieces of fan mail they would get each week. When people recognise me, I don't like it. I don't know them, yet they think they know me.

If being on the TV, in newspapers and magazines is your bread and butter, and you earn tons of money and need to keep that lifestyle going that's your business. That certainly seemed to be the case with a lot of these celebs and personalities.

I remember smiling to myself as they were all talking about their kids in private school. This is not my world, and never has been. Early lockdown, many private schools were taking a more extreme stance in terms of restrictions and closures than state schools. Some celebrities were moaning, saying they were considering taking their children out of the fee-paying schools.

But I'm a *nosy* bugger and found it interesting to get a glimpse into their lifestyles and how lockdown was impacting them. One told me that when they travel on the train, they don't just go first class, they make sure the whole carriage is empty.

Those private conversations, whether in a group on WhatsApp or direct, was a precious time for me, they confirmed that I was going in the right direction in terms of a counter narrative I was offering. It helped me at the time to know everything I was doing was bang on, but, unlike the celebrities, I was able to say it. I wasn't frightened of anyone.

And to answer the obvious question, what about your income Anna, how did you cope?

I always kept this very private, but when I left ITV Central in 2008 I had saved a decent amount of money and started renovating properties and renting them out. It wasn't big money, just enough to cover the bills and I always knew my mum and dad, who were both retired teachers, would help me out if I got desperate. I am blessed with a wonderful supportive family who I always know would help me out financially if I needed it. As long as I could pay for food, water, electric, council tax etc, we would be fine.

I could live without holidays and luxuries, nothing was going to stop me from doing this work. And let's face it, during lockdown there was nothing to spend our money on anyway.

In terms of celebrities, I found some of them to be vacuous, but only in the same way I found the people I used to work with in TV. Those I knew before 2020 were local minor celebs, but they were all a bit odd. They needed the feed of being recognised and the fake adulation you get from fans who don't really know you. Then there are really talented musicians, artists, actors and sports personalities who are famous because they're bloody good at something. Becoming well known is weird and takes a huge amount of adjustment. I only know this as I still get recognised.

What was important about this lockdown Covid period was that people could utilise that celebrity status and recognition to start the debate and spark the conversation that wasn't happening in the MSM.

They were valuable - very valuable and, like I said, I wish I could name them all. Please, if you can remember any of them, take the time to message them and say thank you, because they have only suffered for speaking out; there were no sponsorship deals or contracts for doing this work. Only shame and embarrassment for saying what we were all thinking.

I do know that some of these prominent people went through some horrific experiences, sleepless nights, losing income and work contracts, relationship breakdowns. Let's make sure they know we are grateful for their sacrifice.

There were many celebrities I spoke to "off the record" via the telephone and I can think of three in particular - household names from ITV and the BBC. There are many more who corresponded via written messages. You would all know who they are, but these guys didn't speak out. I think they were in a real dilemma about this and at the time wanted to do more. I am sure they are doing their best to forget it all now, breathe a sigh of relief and glad that the pressure they felt to do something has now gone. I would be in that community, but I must catalogue the insanity we just went through.

You may ask me to name these celebrities, but why would I? It is their business. I think if people don't want to do the decent honourable thing and we all suffer, then we all suffer. It was meant to be. You can't pressure someone into doing something they don't want to do. Yes, more celebrities could have spoken out and made a difference and people I think we all excepted to, sadly, didn't.

You know the type, often from the world of art and music whose very brand and persona is based around rebellion, about protecting important values such as freedom. The characters we thought were anti-establishment and open-minded, free, critical thinkers. People who had a lot of money and some retired with not a lot to lose.

But there have been no consequences for them either. Speaking out meant abuse and smear pieces from MSM and a potential loss of future income. So we must thank and remember those that did do the right thing.

I cannot name all of the celebrities who spoke out for fear of missing anyone out. I would feel terrible if I did. I also can't name those who wanted to speak out and didn't as that was their choice. And I certainly can't name the celebrities who smeared and shamed those for speaking out, as again there are so many.

It was just such an interesting period of our lives that we must look back on and reflect upon. I guess it all comes down to doing the right thing, regardless of the consequences. If there is no benefit to speaking out, why would you? That is, I guess, what will make society strong and united in the future. Doing the right thing for the collective, rather than protecting the self.

Now on to my interview with Robbie Williams in June 2020. This was not focused on Covid or lockdown, vaccines etc, but we touched on it. I only include this in the book as I think it is important and relevant to this chapter.

Why did Robbie talk to me? I had a small following at the time of about 120k across platforms, but he knew I understood "that" community, one that really grew online following the release of the Wikileaks Podesta emails in 2016.

It is a massive subject, and it would take another book to explain it all. But it was clear he watched and listened to everything, like I did. I think he is a very clever guy, who didn't dismiss and reject something without investigation or consideration.

Just because something appears to be completely beyond belief doesn't mean it is.

"There is an alien in the living room, mum."

"Yes, dear," she replied.

Even if the alien was in front of my mum, I am not sure she would believe it was there.

Robbie Williams had the kind of mind I have, one that would think like that. I felt back then that there were three reasons he gave this interview. Firstly, because he wanted to speak directly to that alternative community which he liked and respected. Secondly, he had concerns that this community was going a bit mad, lost as to what is true and what isn't (and I would agree with him there). And thirdly, he wanted to protect his reputation. He had been getting comments that upset and worried him, in relation to certain symbolism in his music and the outfits he had worn in the past.

He is an open, honest and intelligent guy but ultimately I felt that he could only go so far. He was a big name and had some power to derail and destabilise the dominant narrative at the time. I think it must be because he has a family and a very large security bill to pay each year and positive headlines cost money. He is a dad and would have, like me, put his family first.

I think the interview I did with him and the song he released in November 2020 said a lot. Read the lyrics to his single, *You Can't Stop Christmas*.

Thank you, Robbie, for doing what you could. I think he did as much as he could.

CHAPTER SIX - The Doctors

I remember in the early days (May and June 2020) doctors united to form groups that sprung up all around the world. From ACU2020, the Belgium Doctors, Frontline American Doctors, Doctors 4 Covid Ethics, Hart, Panda, World Freedom Alliance, Canada Doctors and many more, the sincerest apologies for those that I have missed. Many more came along in 2021 and 2022.

But this was the first time I encountered censorship on *YouTube*, when I shared ACU2020 and the Belgium Doctors group. It just got removed, I had a strike (three and you lose the channel) but was able to continue with other important interviews. This was early in 2020 when my *YouTube* channel was really taking off.

On July 27th 2020, a live broadcast by *Breitbart News* on *Facebook* was removed, they claimed it was the highest-performing *Facebook* post in the world. It was a press conference in Washington D.C. held by the group America's Frontline Doctors. It has been reported that *YouTube* and *Twitter* also removed footage of this press conference.

And in Germany at the end of August 2020, a protest took place in Berlin. The BBC reported on this, their headline on the 30th August 2020 was, "Germany coronavirus: Anger after attempt to storm parliament - BBC News."

It says: *"An attempt to storm Germany's parliament building during protests against Covid-19 restrictions has been condemned by politicians across the political spectrum.*
Demonstrators, many with far-right sympathies, broke through a cordon and ran up the steps of the parliament building before police dispersed them. The interior minister said there should be "zero tolerance" for such behaviour.
Some 38,000 turned out for the wider, largely peaceful Berlin demonstration. Demonstrators bearing the flag of former imperial Germany - used by the Reichsbürger (Reich Citizens) far-right group - overcame a handful of police to run to the entrance of the Reichstag Building in Berlin. Police put the number involved at several hundred."

I think we can all remember the reporting of these protests on new and old media. I remember very well the first doctors to speak out, from Dr Heiko Schoning and Dr Simone Gold, Prof. Dolores Cahill and Sucharit Bhakdi

MD. Then Dr Mike Yeadon came along, Dr Roger Hodkinson, Dr Robert Malone, Dr Peter McCullough and Dr Ryan Cole. It's interesting to look back and see at what point these individuals came forward. I could write an entire chapter on Dr Mike Yeadon alone. There is no doubt that he was instrumental in fuelling the anger we saw spill out on to the streets in terms of protests. He could talk - other highly respected immunologists, virologists and epidemiologists were also speaking out - but he had the gift of powerful communication. So did Dr Roger Hodkinson. They were powerful orators.

So how did I find out about these people? It would be via email, or *Twitter* and *LinkedIn*. I was overwhelmed with messages without anyone to help me reply and manage the dozens coming through every day, I missed the opportunity to interview many of them who reached out.

I will be honest here, I have always been very stressed about taking on staff. For starters, I didn't have the money, but I had the offer of many volunteers. But what if they replied on my behalf and it wasn't what I would have said? I couldn't copy myself, so at the time I felt it wasn't worth the risk. My reputation and my values are important to me and I didn't have the time to find anyone who could really take the job on. How could I know they would reflect me in terms of their communication to others?

With the kids off school this was a really difficult time for me and I deeply regret not spending more time to focus on them. I felt pulled in two directions dealing with their needs in the present, but also protecting their future in terms of freedom and democracy by fighting this horrific censorship.

I had the celebs/personalities, the grassroots and protest movements and the doctors and journalists to help. There was far too much, but I tried to focus on the interviews and connections I felt would make the biggest difference. And I was acutely aware of how they came across, the consequent impact that would have on how they would be viewed and how I would be viewed. And I say how I would be viewed because, if I messed up, I would lose that credible following I was trying to build. Then I would lose the ability to make a difference in terms of shaping public opinion and perception. I tried to give these experts some advice without causing offence to them or to other new media platforms. I wanted to protect their message and their reputation so it would reach as many people as possible.

For example, many doctors would not turn down an invitation to speak anywhere and everywhere. And I could understand why, from their perspective they were trying to save our future, our children's future, save debate, democracy and save lives. In their minds it was a case of, 'speak to as many people as possible to reach as many people as possible'. Therefore, they would not turn down an invitation to speak on any channel. Prof. Martin Kulldorff, for instance, who was smeared by *The Guardian* for speaking to the small radio channel run by Richie Allen.

Their headline on the 19th October 2020: Anti-lockdown advocate appears on radio show that has featured Holocaust deniers.

So would it then be wise for example for Dr Roger Hodkinson to speak to Richie Allen? Would that dilute the important message he needed to deliver?

I developed a very close friendship and relationship with Dr Roger Hodkinson, and he used to ask my advice on who he should speak to, which I gladly gave. But this caused offence to some content creators and new media organisations, and for this I apologise, but I hope I have explained my reasons for doing this. I also used to ask Dr Roger Hodkinson what he thought of other doctors such as Prof. Dolores Cahill or Dr Mike Yeadon and whether I should be sharing their content. He was always very open and honest with me. I really trusted his view on this as it was not an area I really understood.

It is true though that we were in this world where it was not about the evidence or who was saying it, but who they were saying it to. Would my family, who trusted the BBC for example, listen to Prof. Martin Kulldorff if they had read that Guardian article smear piece?

I've been criticised for advising teachers, or doctors, journalists etc to try the legacy MSM first before new media channels and there is a very good reason for this. If the objective was to increase the reach to the right people, then they needed guidance on who they spoke to. When people see certain media brands, they just turn off, they don't even watch it for 10 seconds.

Which is why I was delighted to see in October 2020 Freddie Sayers help launch the Great

Barrington Declaration. He was the man for the job and did a fabulous one at that.

I was also very careful about the doctors I interviewed, as there were some very high-profile individuals at the start who were getting a lot of attention. Dr Roger Hodkinson helped me with that just as I helped him with which media organisations he should speak to.

Instinctively I learned to avoid interviews with those who appeared to predict something that had not yet happened. That could damage my reputation and theirs in terms of credibility. Specifically, I mean negative predictions regarding a future that had not yet happened. These were not helpful at the time in terms of winning people over. What do I mean by winning people over? Allowing them to feel safe to ask questions. Making sure we don't fall into a community of people who all think the same way as us, which we call an echo chamber.

Some medical professionals handled their media presence very well, others made mistakes. I encouraged them to tone it down, stick to the facts and evidence of what we know today, and avoid speculation and conjecture. Advised them not to express an opinion or conclusion based on incomplete information and evidence. We were all panicking and emotional, angry and scared, so this was a big ask. I think this is why Dr John Campbell has done so well in terms of reach on *YouTube*, he stuck to what do we know today and how do we know it and why should you be interested?

But why would a doctor know or understand public relations or brand reputation? If you trash your brand you trash your ability to earn money and potentially your career. For example, in July 2020, Dr Mohammad Adil was suspended from the UK medical register.

The British Medical Journal reported on the 6th July 2020. *"A consultant surgeon has been suspended from the UK medical register for 12 months pending the outcome of an investigation by the General Medical Council, after posting videos on social media claiming that covid-19 is a hoax.*

Mohammad Iqbal Adil, who qualified in Pakistan, has worked in the NHS for nearly 30 years. He was suspended from the register in June by an interim orders tribunal after claiming in videos on social media platforms and in online interviews that the novel coronavirus has been orchestrated by the elite to control the world.

A GMC spokesperson said, "The interim orders tribunal imposed an interim suspension on Dr Adil's registration, following our referral, to protect patients and public confidence. This interim suspension remains in place while we consider concerns about Dr Adil's fitness to practise."

Some doctors would let loose with all their fears, some of them unfounded, which could easily result in them quickly being called conspiracy theorists. And we have all seen how one wrong statement or tweet is an easy bite for a MSM publication wishing to tarnish and destroy someone's reputation. They didn't listen to these people and, as already mentioned, this must be a stain on their reputation ongoing for not doing so.

For me, I wish I had done more to assist these people in the beginning. It wasn't just what they said, it was who they said it to and it was also about what they shared on their own platforms like *Twitter*. Mistakes could be made in a second; angry and emotional after a couple of glasses of wine you share what feels and looks right not knowing if it really is and those reputations could then never easily be recovered. We call this crisis communications. Something I know a little about, but I am certainly not an expert.

I can share an important example of why I found it important to challenge the MSM, but also work with them. On the 1st July 2020, I did an interview with Cardiff GP Rick O'Shea and former BBC Sports presenter for Scrum V. To my knowledge, he has never shared controversial views on any topic before, but my interview with him focused on children. The wonderful children's focused campaign group UsForThem put me in touch with him and he has remained a good friend since.

Rick spoke about the potential harms on children during lockdown, by missing out on school and other activities such as swimming, playing football and seeing their family and friends. He was the father of two boys and saw how they struggled during lockdown and had the compassion and courage to speak out for other children. He also criticised the BBC and other media brands for not airing alternative views or any kind of counter narrative.

I contacted a journalist I knew at *WalesOnline* who I met when I was working for the National

Union of Journalists Training Wales. She got the green light to run the story and it ended up as front-page news in the *Wales on Sunday* in July 2020.

The headline: "GP calls for schools to be re-opened fully and for lockdown to end." Rick also suffered for speaking out and I look forward one day to doing a follow-up interview with him. He didn't lose his job, although it was a close call.

It is interesting to note that our new prime minister Rishi Sunak was also against closing the schools. I recommend reading The Lockdown Files, published by *The Spectator* in August 2022 for more on this.

So going back to that front page in the *Wales on Sunday*, I was too excited and optimistic at the time that this interview would make a difference and I should have been calmer and more positive about the potential small impact it had. Politicians in Wales didn't read it and say "ok, let's now open the schools", but it at least let a certain audience know that not everyone was on board with lockdown and that a well-respected local doctor had concerns. And it highlighted the fact that we weren't debating the impact lockdown was having on children. I am sure it then encouraged others to speak out, as he was being given valuable airtime with a legacy media brand.

I would expect immediate results and I should have seen it more as chipping away at the establishment or legacy MSM that we all knew and had a relationship of trust with. *Wales on Sunday* is a big deal in Wales, the nation's biggest-selling newspaper and I knew this would reach a different audience. It is the media brand in Wales that many politicians and journalists respect and read and, let's face it, these are the guys who decide the rules of society.

I knew many people who wrote off the MSM, believing they could not work with them or trust them. But that was wrong. There were many journalists willing to publish these stories if they stacked up.

It is important to always think about your purpose and intention and mine was to plant that seed of doubt about the dominant narrative at the time that lockdown was the only path. We needed to discuss the harms lockdown was having on the vulnerable and these publications and journalists were able to reach an audience that I couldn't.

However, I had another story in 2021 where a 12-year-old girl was left at the bus stop because she did not have a mask or a mask exemption card. *WalesOnline* this time didn't run the story because the parent didn't want to be named (at the time I am sure this parent feared the backlash and abuse and I completely understand how they felt). For me, on this occasion, I felt this was the wrong editorial decision. I found this incident very distressing as it occurred close to where I live. The girl was in Year Seven and had just started secondary school. She was three miles from school when the bus came to pick her up, she didn't have a mobile with her and her parents had left for work. Thankfully on this particular occasion she had a house key and could go home and use the landline to call her parents and a neighbour then took her to school.

I did try to get this story into *WalesOnline* but they didn't feel it could be published as the parent did not want to be named. But the reporter confirmed that they believed this incident had taken place. I know this reporter tried their best to get it published.

When I shared this incident on my *Facebook* page, a senior communications professional who had once worked for the BBC spoke up and said that *WalesOnline* had made the wrong decision. She commented underneath my post saying that an anonymity request from the parent would not prevent publication. I agree. There was enough evidence to show the incident had happened and the public needed to know this.

But I know many people gave up on talking to regional media, seeing them as the damaged MSM who had let them down, but I know there were good journalists out there who would have taken the time to listen to and investigate these important stories.

Many just shared their angst on *Twitter* and this unfortunately went ignored by those making the decisions. We get the reaction we want from our echo chamber on *Twitter* when we share our confusion and pain, but it doesn't mean it is making a difference. You are preaching to the converted. Let's go back to what was my purpose and intention of this work. It is to encourage challenge and debate, to shame the MSM for ignoring important voices that needed to be heard.

Jenna Platt, who has grown a large following on Instagram, got the tone right on this. At protests and on her UK tour, she wore a nurse's uniform and a sandwich board declaring "nurses are scared to speak out". She calls herself the nurse who asks questions, wanting to know why we can't debate lockdown or masks. If these things are forced upon us, surely it is insane to not allow a debate around their effectiveness?

Health professionals who had a right to be heard were ignored - and to say they were upset is an understatement, they were distraught. I could see it kept them up all night, dominating their every waking thought. They went into the job to help people and to care for people and now they felt they couldn't. I don't know how but I could pick up on their pain, perhaps from my time training to be a counsellor, I felt immense distress from them. They had no outlet, no platform and I felt it was my duty to come away from the media training and go back into journalism so people could hear what they had to say and make up their own mind.

I suggested that sharing a statement via their LinkedIn profile, that we could all share from there, would be the best option. I know this was the approach of Dr Geert Vanden Bossche, which I think is sensible. This I call direct broadcasting and then there could be no smear pieces, relating to who they had spoken to. I also started interviewing them, beginning in May 2020 with Prof. Robert Endres from Imperial College London who contacted me via Linkedin. I was very nervous about doing these interviews as I had not done anything like it before. I'd been a TV news reporter and presenter, but I had never done long-form interviews.

I also knew it could potentially have an impact on my reputation, as I had an excellent relationship with my corporate clients with lots of work coming in. But how could I say no? How could any journalist in my position say no?

Robert came to me aghast at how the BBC were portraying the pandemic and the subsequent measures imposed by the Government. He was highly critical of Prof. Neil Ferguson's modelling report. So on the 30th May 2020 we spoke and that's how my journey started.

Prof. Robert Endres also from Imperial College London, is a professor in systems biology and leads the biological physics group. Did this person not have a right to be heard, to enter the debate around Prof. Neil Ferguson's controversial modelling report? If the BBC weren't going to speak to him, I had to. I asked

Robert to leave me a review on Linkedin in order to attract other academics of his calibre to come forward. I wanted them to know that I would allow them to view and, if necessary, ask for edits of the interview before publication and that it would be handled in a professional manner. So many new media channels were not run by qualified journalists. I wanted to make sure these guests knew I would handle them sensitively.

Dr Roland Salmon may have not had the celebrity following that, for example, Dr Mike Yeadon later had, but he is a former director of communicable diseases for Public Health Wales. In October 2021, he said lockdowns should not be brought back in.

From a BBC News article published on the 22nd October 2021,
"Covid lockdown restrictions should not be brought back to help NHS Wales deal with winter pressures, a former health boss has said.

Dr Roland Salmon, former director of communicable diseases for Public Health Wales, said he believed such rules were only "at best marginally" beneficial.

He said efforts should be redoubled to vaccinate those most at risk."

In Feb 2022 he called for a pause to the rollout of vaccines for children:

From a WalesOnline article published on the 16th February 2022, "Former Welsh public health chief calls for pause to rollout of vaccine for children.

A group of doctors and scientists has called for a pause to the roll out of the Covid vaccine for children and teenagers saying the risk outweighs benefits which they claim are now "virtually zero".

Among them is Dr Roland Salmon, former director of the communicable disease centre in Wales. He said the timing of Welsh Government's further announcement on February 15 that all children aged 5 to 11 will be offered the Covid jab was "extraordinary".

Dr Roland Salmon was retired but would have been called on to be a media spokesperson for Public Health Wales had he still been in employment at the time the Covid crisis hit. He was calm, reasonable and balanced, sticking to what we know now rather than predicting a future that had not yet happened. He didn't touch on people's fears and anxieties in terms of the crazy behaviour we were seeing from our governments and how that made us all panic and then betting on what our future may look like.

We saw individuals such as Dr Salmon get a voice in the old media brands like the BBC and the *Daily Mail* but it wasn't sustained. It was not a campaign, but the odd article here and there. Please don't think that the news is the news. These media organisations have campaigns, stories they focus on for weeks, months and years on end like Harry and Meghan. But this one was fear - it was pumped out as the headline day in and day out.

I liked the team at Public Health Wales where Dr Salmon had worked. I had been delighted to give them media training in 2019, showing them how to film and edit at speed on their mobiles. They were one of my first clients. Prof. Martin Kulldorff again was a giant in terms of academic credibility, but his delivery was straight and quiet.

The issue was Dr Mike Yeadon and Dr Roger Hodkinson are powerful communicators, the way they passionately executed their message was different. Then followed Dr Robert Malone and Dr Ryan Cole. Also Dr Simone Gold who was vocal from the start. They were good at connecting with scared people. Then those who bring in the feelings and emotions of the viewer and touch them in a way that they never forget, touch their fears in terms of an unknown future. I was more like Yeadon, Gold and Hodkinson. Do I regret this? Yes and no. It got more people to listen, but I was pulled into voicing and repeating predictions. But when we see crazy behaviour that makes no sense from those democratically elected, this inevitably leads us on to further assumptions about a future we are losing confidence in.

To the brave doctors who spoke out, I wish I could celebrate you all. You had something important to say that we were not allowed to hear. It was never about you being right or wrong, it was about the insanity that we weren't allowed to hear it and you were brave enough to say it.

The future will not look bright without trust and we won't have trust if we don't allow debate. Just to shut these people up as conspiracy nuts was never going to be a strong sell for any media organisation, old or new. And I say new media because they didn't listen to those who didn't agree with them either. If we are demanding debate from the MSM and then don't deliver it with the new media, then we are just as bad. We need to listen to all, allowing debate with opposing voices is the only option in my opinion in terms of a bright future, for society, for cohesion and for democracy to thrive.

If journalists such as Jeremy Vine from the BBC does not want protestors turning up at his home, he needs to bring in real balance and debate to his content. If BBC Disinformation Reporter Marianna Spring wants to build trust in her media brand, she needs to understand and represent all voices. The BBC didn't talk to the protestors and now I don't think it would be safe for them to; I am guessing they would get a lot of verbal abuse. But if they had gone to the first few protests in 2020 they would have been welcomed.

It is important to note that in October 2020 Dr Mike Yeadon was given a full-page article in *The Daily Mail*, but, after that, speaking to journalists "off the record", they felt he had lost his way in terms of predicting an unknown future.

The article published on the 30th October 2020 reads: Three facts No 10's experts got wrong: DR MIKE YEADON says claims that the majority of the population is susceptible to Covid, that only 7% are infected so far and virus death rate is 1% are all false.

I was going to interview Dr Mike Yeadon again in 2021 but I explained to him that I had got in touch with his former colleagues and wanted to challenge him with this information. I had read the *Reuters Special Report* published on the 18th March 2021 the title was "The ex-Pfizer scientist who became an anti-vax hero."

It reads: *"Michael Yeadon was a scientific researcher and vice president at drugs giant Pfizer Inc. He co-founded a successful biotech. Then his career took an unexpected turn.*

Late last year, a semi-retired British scientist co-authored a petition to Europe's medicines regulator. The petitioners made a bold demand: Halt COVID-19 vaccine clinical trials.

Even bolder was their argument for doing so: They speculated, without providing evidence, that the vaccines could cause infertility in women.

The document appeared on a German website on Dec.1. Scientists denounced the theory. Regulators weren't swayed, either: Weeks later, the European Medicines Agency approved the European Union's first COVID-19 shot, co-developed by Pfizer Inc. But damage was already done.

Social media quickly spread exaggerated claims that COVID-19 jabs cause female infertility. Within weeks, doctors and nurses in Britain began reporting that concerned women were asking them whether it was true, according to the Royal College of Obstetricians & Gynaecologists. In January, a survey by the Kaiser Family Foundation (KFF), a non-profit organization, found that 13% of unvaccinated people in the United States had heard that "COVID-19 vaccines have been shown to cause infertility."

What gave the debunked claim credibility was that one of the petition's co-authors, Michael Yeadon, wasn't just any scientist. The 60-year-old is a former vice president of Pfizer, where he spent 16 years as an allergy and respiratory researcher. He later co-founded a biotech firm that the Swiss drugmaker Novartis purchased for at least $325 million."

Further down the article it talks about his former colleagues.

"According to Yeadon's LinkedIn profile, he joined Pfizer in 1995; the company had a large operation then in Sandwich in southern England. He rose to become a vice president and head of allergy and respiratory research.

Many former colleagues say they are baffled by his transformation.

Mark Treherne, chairman of Talisman Therapeutics in Cambridge, England, said he overlapped with Yeadon at Pfizer for about two years and sometimes had coffee with him. "He always seemed knowledgeable, intelligible, a good scientist. We were both trained as pharmacologists … so we had something in common."

"I obviously disagree with Mike and his recent views," he said. Treherne's company is researching brain inflammation, which he said could be triggered by coronaviruses. "This does not sound like the guy I knew 20 years ago."

Moschos, the ex-colleague who took issue with one of Yeadon's tweets, said he considered him a mentor when they worked together at the drugmaker from 2008 to 2011. More recently, Moschos has been researching whether it's possible to test for COVID-19 with breath samples. He said Yeadon's views are "a huge disappointment." He recounted hearing Yeadon in a radio interview last year.

"There was a tone in his voice that was nothing like I ever remembered of Mike," Moschos said. "It was very angry, very bitter."

John LaMattina, a former president of Pfizer Global Research and Development, also knew Yeadon. "His group was very successful and discovered a number of compounds that entered early clinical development," LaMattina told Reuters in an email. He said Yeadon and his team were let go by Pfizer, however, when the company made the strategic decision to exit the therapeutic area they were researching.

LaMattina said he had lost touch with Yeadon in recent years. Shown links to Yeadon's video declaring the pandemic over and a copy of his petition to halt COVID-19 clinical trials, LaMattina replied: "This is all news to me and a bit of a shock. This seems out of character for the person I knew."

So I read the entire article and then I emailed those quoted and they got back to me with questions I wanted to put to Mike. He may have considered them to be trivial, ridiculous and insulting, but he declined to do the interview. He would have reached more people had he done it. His power to deliver an important message would have grown had he accepted that challenge.

Everyone shouts at me, 'pick a side Anna'. How dare you read this Reuters article and even give time to those who were critical of Dr Mike Yeadon. Well doesn't that make me just as bad as the people who we were angry with? For not listening to both sides?

I did have a side though; my side was the children. They were suffering and, as hard as I found it to be balanced and calm, I couldn't. Because they were suffering and continue to suffer. But here I at least explain why I couldn't be calm about the future, or that balanced, listening journalist deep down I wanted to be, the one I knew could make a real difference, the one I wanted to be. You reach into someone's heart, you hear their hopes and dreams, their fears. You can communicate and you can build a future where everyone is heard.

CHAPTER SEVEN - Global 150 opinions

I gave over my *YouTube* channel to the people - masked up and unable to protest, this was a perfect way to hear from them. Many were sharing on their own platforms, but this was a way of bringing everyone's views together. I remember vividly how this all came about. I was in a small Tesco's supermarket in Cardiff Bay on the 24th July 2020 and, while customers didn't have to wear masks, the staff did. I was served by someone at the checkout who had a mask on. I had always been able to communicate with people as a journalist but now I couldn't. "Do you have to wear that all day, are Tesco forcing you to? What is it like?" I asked.

He mumbled and I couldn't hear him. But he had sad eyes.

I thought, 'right this is totally wrong' and went and bought a sim card the next day. I had an old Samsung phone that I only needed for my courses which had stopped during lockdown. I went on *YouTube* and all of my other channels and asked people to start sending in their opinions to this mobile via WhatsApp.

Messages started to flood in. I wanted to make sure the public knew these people were real. I made sure they stated their full name, their occupation, date of publication and their age. I cannot tell you how many people have come up to me and said this saved them. They felt they were going mad, yet these brave, wonderful people sent me their videos. And I published as many as I could. I was struggling to keep on top of the messages I was receiving.

Richard Dale, who went on to run our againstvaccinepassports.com website and helped with the Together Declaration and many others, sent me a video and I was so busy I struggled to see it and he got angry with me. He took the time to record a video and I was so overwhelmed I was missing some. Thankfully I saw his message and was able to publish it, it is on my YouTube channel. The title is Richard Dale, 46, Web Developer, West Yorkshire. 21st August 2020.

I have to say sorry to so many people who emailed me or sent a video. I was on my own, I didn't take on staff as I was scared that they would not reply the way I would have wanted to reply. I needed to be sure I was not smeared or potentially at risk of attack from the MSM, they were going for me, watching my every move. So on my own I tried to handle the 20-30 video messages that I was getting via Whatsapp every day.

The farmer in Scotland, the mother in Essex, the young woman who had decided she could no longer take the risk of having children. Real people from all over the world, masked up, not able to see close family and friends stuck in their homes finally had a way to communicate with others. Reading this in 2022 you need to remember there was no vaccine then, this was about lockdown and the mask mandate.

These people had given up on old established media brands who were pumping out this insane one-sided narrative. They were lonely, struggling and suffering and I had a way to give them an outlet. They came in from America, Australia and beyond. It was the most powerful and incredible form of journalism I have ever been involved in. But more than this, I felt I was recording the most important period in our history.

They spoke to and for us all, they captured the moment we were all in. I knew if I spoke and did interviews then it was the Anna Brees Show, about how I was struggling, but this was their story. I was finally able to hear their pain from behind the mask. That man who worked in Tesco in Cardiff Bay started it all. His sad eyes, he had to wear a mask, that was the problem - he HAD to wear it. I realised there was a voice that wasn't being heard. That was real journalism - the voice of the people.

I lost my *YouTube* channel on Christmas Day 2020, appealed, then got it back. But then in April 2021, while covering a protest in central London, I lost it again. But in June 2022 after about 20 appeals, I got it back again. I was so happy – not so much to get back all those interviews with doctors, but the global opinions from 2020. That was history, a moment in time that I thought we had lost forever but it is thankfully still there.

Many people would send me video messages that again predicted a future that had not yet happened and I had a difficult time in turning people down. They talked about the monetary system, how it was all going to collapse. Or about how we all needed to prepare - they call them preppers, get food, water source and shelter, prepare to live without an income or security - buy a gun.

I didn't publish these, in the same way I held back from the doctors who predicted a future that had not yet happened. We needed to deal with today. We needed to hear from people who could reflect how we felt today and how we could focus on a future - new media and new government organisations that actually listen to us - as impossible that may now seem, that was our way out of this.

We all have a place now in society. We are all able to make a difference with our words and our passion for the future. We are not alone, we saw this incredible bravery from the global 150 to speak out for us all. I have only had one person who emailed me in June 2022 to ask I remove their interview. They had a job and others didn't understand their position and they were worried about being out of work again. Of course, I removed it. But they know we must have that full spectrum of voices to survive as a society.

That work I did - and we did - was a moment in history we must never forget. They spoke, we listened - and without listening we have no future. That was the only protest I felt we could have at the time; we all forget that to protest was illegal. See this from the 14th February 2022 from the Brighton based Argus newspaper and what happened to Louise.

It reads: "A WOMAN has been fined more than £20,000 for breaching Covid-19 restrictions by holding anti-lockdown protests in London.

Louise Creffield, the founder of Save Our Rights UK, was found guilty on two counts of holding a gathering of more than 50 people on May 29 and June 26 last year.

At the time of the offences, the country was under level three lockdown restrictions, meaning no more than 30 people could meet at once.

The 35-year-old was found to have held gatherings in Hyde Park and Parliament Square in May, before returning for a different protest in Parliament Square in June."

CHAPTER EIGHT - The Journalists

I made sure I spoke to journalists from MSM brands as they still had and still have so much power. Journalists such as David Rose, who had worked on *The Guardian*, *The Observer* and the BBC and was freelance at *The Mail on Sunday* at the time. (David and I had dealings in the past, due to his coverage of the Jersey children's home Haut de la Garenne, but that is another story for another time.) He appeared to be anti-lockdown but pro-vaccine.

He talked to me about how health correspondents from organisations like the BBC may have had to toe the line to get access, dealing with demanding and difficult communications teams which subsequently shapes the content we see. He also spoke alongside Dr Pierre Kory and Dr Tess Lawrie about ivermectin.

I also spoke to Sue Cook on the 6th October 2020, former presenter for flagship shows at the BBC such as *Crimewatch UK* and *Children in Need*. She said after 20 years of listening to the *Today* programme on BBC Radio 4, "I had to turn it off a few months ago, I don't know what's happened to the BBC."

This interview went viral, with hundreds of thousands of views across my channels.

Later, towards the end of 2021, I interviewed Mark Sharman. A former director of broadcasting with *BskyB* with responsibility for *Sky One*, *Sky News* and *Sky Movies*. He was also director of ITV's network and regional news. He was behind the signing of news presenters such as ITV's Julie Etchingham, who had of course like many others been a part of peddling this one-sided narrative. Not picking her out at all, there were hundreds of TV news presenters just reading the autocue and doing nothing to help publish important voices asking for debate.

But I couldn't really get it, how could we have more faith in news presenters than people like Prof. Martin Kulldorff, who at the time was a professor of medicine at Harvard Medical School? Well, that was the insanity of it all wasn't it? How journalists and presenters could get up in the morning and do their job was beyond me. They knew there weren't just a few crackpot doctors who had concerns. And there weren't even hundreds - there were thousands.

So like my interview with Sue Cook and David Rose, I knew an interview with Mark Sharman would penetrate a different type of audience. I could reach journalists and those who only watched the likes of ITV and Sky News, two organisations Mark once had responsibility for.

I can and do regularly put myself in other people's shoes, the people who thought "but it is not on the news, it's on *Facebook*, that doesn't count". A naive view, you might think, but if you don't understand how a story flows from communication and PR departments to MSM, you wouldn't question it. You would just think, "the news is the news."

You may also assume if there was a valid argument that needed to be heard, our wonderful journalists would ensure that happened. After all isn't that their job?

I was hoping that my interview with Mark Sharman would penetrate this particular audience and I believe it did. Mark didn't want to go on camera, he prefers to be behind the scenes. But he is a brave and compassionate man and forced himself to do it.

A senior TV news executive watched our interview. I am not going to say who this person is, but someone described to me that they had probably the most powerful job in daytime TV. I believe this person knew Mark or knew of him.

During our interview, Mark had said the mainstream media had lost its moral compass. I know how a certain statement can touch a nerve, it can sit with you all day, you try and brush it off. You go to bed and hope the next day when you wake it has left you. But this person, who has probably one of the most influential jobs in television, couldn't shift it. Mark Sharman was well regarded and at the most senior level as a news executive at ITV and Sky. Coming from him, it mattered. That statement "the mainstream media has lost its moral compass" is not an easy one to forget.

A few days later I had an email from them. A ranting email, written in the evening and not particularly calm and professional. I spoke to a journalist friend about this and she said that I had clearly touched a nerve. I think they were angry and felt ashamed. I just hope that, if this person does read this book, they actually do something if we as a nation ever go through that insanity of lockdown again. I ended up having a one-hour zoom call with this person and they were very reasonable and open with me. I know their views on lockdown and vaccinating children now. Let's just say this certainly didn't come across in their content.

Now we move to other people who got in touch with me and I think this one is significant. This person described themselves as being on the top table at the BBC. I am happy to share what they said without revealing who they are.

The connection came via someone who followed me and this is the email correspondence we had. I only received two emails of significance which you can read below.

May 2021

Hi Anna
Good to hear from you. X mentioned you, I wasn't familiar but now after googling you I see you're in the business. X is one of my oldest and dearest but the world of X is miles away from news so they don't always get how cutthroat things can be, I'm sure you understand.

I'm a Senior Editor and not to put a fine point on it I need to know who shares our concerns. It's impossible to be up front in top level meetings without knowing who's in with us, and it's not like you can just come out and ask, try that and people look at you like you have two heads.

So it would be helpful if you let me know if you have the ear of anyone in News. I'm not talking about researchers or Strictly Come Dancing *runners, I'm only interested in journalists and editors. Not conspiracy types either, though I doubt there are many of those in NBH. You wonder why we don't cover those protests, it's because of the people with posters of Bill Gates eating aborted foetus. Not going to win many fans.*

I don't do WhatsApp either - massive security risk and people don't even realise.

So you can get people to email me or just let me know who they are if I have any allies in the room. I don't name names.

Now what I can do for you - obviously I can help with internal info if you let me know what you are after.

The first thing you should know is that a story from Health will go up later today/into overnight, the headline will be 'I would have the vaccine again'. An interview with a X, this is stage one of the counter. This should be of interest to you and also serve as proof, in case you had any shred of doubt, that I've got a seat at the top table and can organise the pushback.

This story later went live on BBC Health so I knew they were genuine. I knew they worked at the BBC. Clearly at this point I was concerned this was a phishing exercise; they wanted me to reveal my contacts at the BBC. I relayed my concerns to them and this was their response.

May 2021

Anna, I don't blame you for being cautious, I would be very cautious in your situation. Please have anyone on your side give me a tap on the shoulder, as long as they are on the level.

Your idea is sound, I just need to think through all the implications front and back. Give me a sense of your reach and audience. I'll think about it after I deal with today - be in touch next week.

Further contact I had from the person who put me in touch with this individual came via WhatsApp.

27th May 2021

Major op here, people are running scared. There was an emergency meeting on the 4th floor NBH today, the DG and others. Strategy about who's involved and who to shut out. Teams have been instructed to find out who's with and who's against. What a shitshow.

Another WhatsApp message I received the same day.

There's going to be an urgent meeting tomorrow 10.30. I have the Zoom. Kinda busy but important so I'll be there. If Anna is for real she will know the kind of people who are involved. I can get you some more info but I need to know who in the room I can trust – who is on our side – and who is not. So let me know what top-level people are in the groups you are talking about. Not researchers or strictly runners, reporters and editors. Talk after xx

I am sorry but I won't name these people despite the abuse I may get. These were the good guys, "good" only in that they felt they could make important changes from within and I can't continue to do any good if I name them. I can only be here to listen to them should they come forward again.

What I can confirm is that I sent an email to the BBC Press office asking if they would like to respond to this, giving them a deadline. As I have said many times, new media channels, citizen journalists fail to get a right of reply. If you don't get one let your audience know. I can confirm I didn't get a response.

I continued to stay in contact with this insider at the BBC and the person who put me in contact with them, but after these two emails I didn't hear from them again. Trust was lost and I understand why as I threatened to expose them, even though I had no intention of ever doing so. I wanted a closer relationship with them and it backfired. I have learnt a lot from this. It seems an obvious route, but people don't like being threatened. You have to flatter them and work with them. Make them understand how you see the situation and understand how they see the situation. Gentle and kind pressure to "do the right thing" would have been a better approach.

During that first initial contact, my idea was for them to leak the real true conversations about what was going on at the BBC, as protestors stood outside and shouted shame on you, outside the BBC buildings in Cardiff, Manchester and London - all on the same day. I knew many journalists felt that shame and I wanted to know what was really happening and this person could have leaked a daily or weekly journal about this.

That's pretty intense isn't it? Reading it back now and not knowing whether or not to share this email was a horrifically difficult decision. I needed guidance and a mentor but at the time didn't really have one. I did ask an old boss, someone I used to work with at ITV but, after a good year of conversation, he simply stopped responding. Journalism only goes so far it seems.

But I did discuss this with the other BBC staff I knew at the time who were sharing their thoughts and feelings with me. Why and when would you ever betray confidentiality and trust? I tried what this person suggested and let the other BBC staff know. But there was not enough trust to connect them. They felt this could have been a phishing exercise and the sole intention was to locate and remove those who were not towing the line.

I always look back and wonder why the BBC staff who were unhappy couldn't find a way to connect with each other and form a powerful group to put pressure on the corporation from within. Maybe they did, but we didn't really see the results of that reflected on our TV screens. We needed them to come out publicly on social media, to cause a serious headache for bosses at the BBC. A strong, united group that could put a few cracks in their foundations, like a small bomb going off in the basement and the walls start to crumble. I've seen how courage is infectious; how an idea can take off. How unrest within an organisation can turn into powerful reform. They could have done it. If I were still at the BBC I would have done it. But for whatever reason it didn't happen.

These two tweets sum up the insanity quite beautifully. There had been many protests outside the BBC in Manchester, Cardiff and London in 2021 and 2022. But I am going to talk about the 22nd of January 2022 as I was able to broadcast video/stills from inside and outside the BBC's New Broadcasting House in London. This is the image that you see on the front cover of this book.

I cannot begin to imagine the shame they must have felt as journalists to see that anger and desperation coming from the British public and to completely ignore them. Journalists are not fools, they know that the public are their bread and butter, their raison d'etre is to serve them. Those former colleagues of mine at the BBC had to just hang their heads in shame and keep quiet. I cannot imagine how difficult that must have been.

There were two tweets that summed up this madness. Take time if you can, and search these up on my Twitter feed.

On the 22nd January 2022. A loud and angry crowd gather outside BBC's new broadcast house in central London against vaccine passports and vaccine mandates.

And also on the 22nd January 2022, a photo which is the front cover of this book, taken inside BBC New Broadcasting House

Their tiny act of rebellion I am imagining was to take that photo. I was told that it was passed around BBC staff communication groups on WhatsApp. This must have been the first time in the history of the BBC that they ignored a huge volume of voices that had spilled out on to the streets wanting to be heard.

Well, I did get an idea of how some journalists felt, contacts I spoke to off the record at the BBC, ITV, Sky and a couple of employees who work for Reach plc. I will never forget in

September 2020 when covering a London protest, I was approached by a reporter from a well-known broadsheet newspaper. It was a day I remember very well. I got lost trying to find a tube station on the outskirts of London, so ended up driving straight into central London. I parked as close as I could to Trafalgar Square and found a spot by the Ritz Hotel, which was an eye-watering £15 an hour. I didn't stay long, but I needed to capture the pain of the nation and hear the voices that were being ignored.

This reporter said, 'well done for what you are doing, I follow you on *Twitter* and I am a bit ashamed of what they are trying to ask me to do in covering this event'. This gives you an idea of the kind of coverage we were hearing at the time.

19th Sept 2020 from *The Independent*, Trafalgar Square protest: Conspiracy theorists clash with police at anti-lockdown demonstration.

It reads: *"Hundreds of conspiracy theorists have gathered in central London to protest against coronavirus restrictions in the UK as infections worsen.*

Scuffles broke out as police moved in on demonstrators in Trafalgar Square, who formed human blockades in an attempt to prevent arrests and initially forced officers to move back.

Demonstrators advanced on police while shouting "choose your side" and some were seen throwing objects at officers during a largely peaceful demonstration on Saturday afternoon.

At around 3pm, the Metropolitan Police announced that it would be dispersing protesters and making arrests after trying to "explain, engage and encourage them to leave throughout" the day."

I was lucky in that I could throw myself into the protest crowd and reflect accurately the people who were there. I wasn't sent to smear like many who had been sent with that brief.

In an interview with Prof. Richard Ennos from the University of Edinburgh on the 11th September 2020, he explains how a BBC reporter admitted to him that she was sent to smear protestors at a rally in Edinburgh on the 5th September as part of the Saving Scotland Group.

So how did journalists deal with being asked to do this, how did they wake up in the morning, jump out of bed with excitement and enthusiasm about the important job they had to do as the fourth estate?

These journalists tell themselves that they are doing their best - with bills to pay they must weigh it all up. I think they numb that spirit within them that cares about debate, challenge and democracy and I am afraid they are putting their children's future at risk.

I can imagine they were seeing and speaking to Covid patients day in and day out. They weren't like me getting dozens of emails a week from horrified professors and doctors calling for lockdown to end. I think they tricked themselves into thinking they were doing the right thing, or focused on paying the mortgage and putting food on the table. I know because I spoke to some of them. They could not risk losing their income. That is very sad, but that is what we need to make sure does not happen again.

There are many MSM journalists, and people working in communications who contacted me. Some I can name, some I can't. But we did connect and communicate and we tried our best to fight this horrific one-sided beast of a narrative being pumped through our TV screens every day. So much shame - I really felt it, so much embarrassment and shame for a profession we once felt so proud to be a part of. Those who stayed quiet, but knew deep down what they were doing was wrong had to compartmentalise that shame. They just removed it from their psyche, it was the only way they could carry on pumping out the crap that the misfortunate, ignorant public were bombarded with day in day out.

CHAPTER NINE - Censorship

I have spoken a little already about censorship and how it was the catalyst in terms of my return to content creating and journalism. Starting with Dan Erikson and Artin Massihi the Californian doctors in their navy tunics and the video of their press conference that went viral on *YouTube* with 5.46 million views, in April 2020.

This was simply the beginning, and why people didn't fight at the first point I do not know. That was when we were in danger, immediately I knew if you censor credible medical professionals who had something important to impart it was not going to be a good start to this public health emergency. We were not privy to the full spectrum of voices with an alternative view. Had we have been, life would look very different here in 2022.

We see the BBC's coverage of vaccine injury and death, so very different to GB News. For example, compare the Mark Steyn programme broadcast on the 13th July 2022 on GB News. Again I recommend taking a look at this broadcast which is on their YouTube channel. The title is, Mark Steyn opens his one-off special, where we tell the stories of vaccine-damaged patients and their families.

Then a few days later, on the 16th July 2022 this was published by the *Daily Mail* about a BBC documentary aired that month.

The headline reads: *"A BBC team spent a week trying to convince seven anti-vaxxers to get the Covid jab, amid their claims 'it contains deadly microchips' and is a 'plot to depopulate the Earth': So did any of them change their mind?"*

Would this immense division in terms of two media brands publishing such conflicting content have happened had journalists from day one shouted from the roof tops about those first doctors being removed from *YouTube*, had they pushed into the protest crowds and questioned why people were there?

We could have lived in a world, where the individual is allowed to watch, consider and process the evidence in front of them to make the right decision in terms of their health, rather than being treated like children. It feels like when I watch BBC broadcasts I am seven years old watching *Blue Peter* or *Newsround* again. The way the Government speaks to me, it is as if I am a child. No level of nuance can be tolerated, neither the BBC or the Government will allow me to be a grown up and make up my own mind.

This is the info we have available to us, let's leave it up to you guys to decide, would surely be the adult approach and one I had happily gotten used to in the past.

Day one of censorship from *YouTube* turned into where we are now, which is about day 900 as I come to finishing this book. Important, credible, highly thought of, experts in their field were taken off not only the older legacy media brands, but new global platforms such as *YouTube* and *Twitter*.

Some have survived - if we look at Dr John Campbell or Drbeen Medical Lectures and their recent broadcasts on the efficacy of the Covid vaccination. These *YouTube* accounts have survived, so many haven't. No one really understands why. But I would suggest it is because they have a history of being balanced and they have continued to be balanced.

I have very strange relationships with *Facebook*, *Twitter*, and *YouTube*, in terms of what they allowed me to publish and what they did not. For example, Dr Roger Hodkinson was removed within a few minutes from my

YouTube channel and Dr Tess Lawrie and Dr Mike Yeadon from *Facebook* again within a few hours. I learnt to understand and feel what would be allowed and what wouldn't and from whom.

I had an interesting relationship with all three new global media platforms. *Twitter* was undoubtedly tne best in allowing me to share Dr Tess Lawrie, Dr Robert Malone and Dr Mike Yeadon. *Facebook* were the second best, then *YouTube* were undoubtedly the worst in my experience.

But I know others have had the reverse situation. I believe Dr John Campbell had issues with *Twitter* but has a huge channel on *YouTube*. And recently Dr Anthony Hinton, a regular on GB News and an NHS consultant of nearly 40 years, lost his *Twitter* account in July 2022.

UK primary school headteacher Mike Fairclough had similar problems and faced a seven-day ban for a tweet he published on child vaccination against Covid. In 2022, US virologist Dr Robert Malone was removed from *Twitter* as was founder of PANDA (Pandemics Data & Analytics) Actuary Nick Hudson. At the time of writing, they may now be back on *Twitter*.

Many have appealed but, on many occasions, I have been shocked by *Twitter* censorship even though I have not personally encountered it.

I would observe others and got an idea of what would be allowed and what wouldn't. It was like a game, but the rules were ill-defined. It felt like a dance, a play between different platforms trying my best to get that important counter narrative out there, to make sure people were informed. I will reiterate, it wasn't that these people were necessarily right, it was that they needed to be heard. And as already mentioned my content was not balanced, I put out one view. The view that we weren't hearing.

I tried to get those with opposing views to speak to me, but without success. Talking to the communication departments of these organisations I would usually get no reply. I hope after writing this book that situation changes.

I know this has happened with alternative new media too. I am sure you have noticed that every interview or podcast the guest seems to be treated like a friend. There is no challenge or grilling of the guests. I will give you an example. If you watch almost every interview with David Icke, he is called a hero, a friend, an inspiration and that all of his predictions from the last 30 years have finally come true. Does anyone challenge him when he says vaccinated children will struggle to have children in the future? I heard him say this recently. The host does not challenge this, they don't say, 'How do you know this, where is the evidence?'

Or the Milton Keynes funeral director John O'Looney on Brand New Tube, who recently said:

"Hospitals are covering up baby deaths by cremating babies themselves."

I called John, he didn't have any concrete evidence to stack this up. He seems like a genuinely kind and caring bloke, but you simply can't scare people like this without concrete evidence.

I don't think these people realise the damage they can potentially create in terms of leaving people very cynical and confused. I don't think that was ever their intention, but it is very much an "anything goes" type of environment on *Brand New Tube* and *Rumble*, *Telegram* and *Bitchute* etc.

So as a journalist whether old or new media, you ask, 'where is the evidence to back up this claim. Do you have two sources? Have you checked it out thoroughly and can you back it up and have you gone to the individual or organisation and asked for a response to these allegations?' That is powerful and elevates your post.

There is a feeling of friendship and comradery in the *Telegram* comms groups from the likes of White Rose chat, The Great Re-opening and the many Stand in the Park community groups. I get the vibe that there is an embarrassment to say, 'that may not be true'.

I see all manner of things discussed in these groups and I am sure those reading this who understand those communities, get this. From chemtrails and vaccinated people being locatable via Bluetooth, the Queen is already dead and has been replaced by a clone. (this was written before the Queen died) I could go on, who am I to say this is not true, who am I to say it is true?

But there has certainly been a horrific lack of decent journalism and challenge in the alternative media world. And any WhatsApp group I am in seems to descend into a black hole, of everything is true and please don't offend me by saying I am wrong. Communication groups are friendship groups, these people have been through a lot together. It is therefore embarrassing and awkward to say, 'well I don't agree with that'.

But when I did interviews - and I need to be honest here - it was incredibly difficult to ask the tough, challenging questions without offending a community who trust me. I had a lot of abuse - and it was horrific. I was earning a lot less money doing this work, not really enjoying it and getting a lot of grief. I felt I had to do it for the sake of democracy, our children and our future.

But the abuse was horrific and I would constantly be called a shill, grifter, controlled opposition, a traitor, and all manner of swear words. So I was scared to ask those difficult questions as I am far more delicate than I think people realise.

But I saw those impassioned pleas from the likes of Yeadon and Lawrie and shared them. They of course went viral within that community, and I contributed to it - people who held on to their truth and ignored all other views.

That lack of a middle ground is dangerous and here in July 2022 I am seeing very clearly what a mess these media organisations, old and new, are responsible for.

If you can discredit those speaking out against lockdown, masks and vaccines, rather than bring them into debate – both sides are losing, both sides are screaming that they are right and cannot deal with challenge. No one - not old or new media – has made it fair, don't pit three against one, pit two against two. Isn't that what we are all so desperate for? The problem, as already mentioned, is that people see their media brand like a friend and not one to challenge. That is why that boring middle ground none of us find very exciting and engaging, doesn't seem to exist. It tells us that we might be wrong, so people switched off from it.

I look back now and saw how many migrated to *Telegram* for example after witnessing the toxic behaviours of *Facebook*, *YouTube* and Twitter from removing these important counter narratives. But I also think these organisations would have been under enormous pressure.

In particular, I remember the interview between Dr. Anthony Fauci and Facebook CEO Mark Zuckerberg, on the 16th July 2020.

In my opinion, Mark Zuckerberg does not look comfortable in this broadcast. Again you can watch it on YouTube via the Reuters channel.

Could it be that *Facebook* were told they had to publish only the Government narrative or they would be punished in some way, even removed?

How do we know what Mark Zuckerberg really thought? I do remember him saying the following, as reported in The Washington Times on the 17th February 2021.

"Facebook CEO Mark Zuckerberg has banned from his social media platforms any claims that the novel coronavirus vaccine alters DNA, although he himself expressed similar concerns last year.
Project Veritas released video Tuesday of Mr. Zuckerberg raising questions about whether vaccines include risks of side effects such as "modifying people's DNA and RNA" in July during a virtual Q&A meeting with staff.
"I do just want to make sure that I share some caution on this because we just don't know the long-term side effects of basically modifying people's DNA and RNA to directly code in a person's DNA and RNA," Mr. Zuckerberg said in the video. "Basically the ability to produce

those antibodies and whether that causes other mutations or other risks downstream."

Also on the 17th February another media publication, the Israel National News published an article saying; "Facebook CEO Mark Zuckerberg takes "anti-vax" stance in violation of own policy. Zuckerberg: "I share some caution on this, because we just don't know the long-term side effects of basically modifying people's DNA, RNA."

I had been in touch with Alex Belardinelli, Comms Director for Northern Europe for Meta (previously known as *Facebook*). He was open to discussion at one point.

I also interviewed now President for Global Affairs at Meta, Nick Clegg, during my time at ITV Central and really liked him. This is when he was Lib Dem MP for Sheffield Hallam. I had to get a soundbite from him for the ITV national news. I got a really good vibe from him. Many disliked him after the decision the Lib Dems made over tuitions fees, they said they would not bring them in. But in a collation with the Conservative Government in 2010 the party did a huge U-turn.

To remind you, read this from the *Independent* from the 9th December 2019.

"It has been nine years since the Lib Dems betrayed students over tuition fees – don't let them fool you again.

In the 2010 general election, the Liberal Democrats built their campaign around a pledge to abolish tuition fees. By the end of that year, however, they had tripled them instead."

Here I go back to compromise and balance. The Lib Dems had entered a coalition with the Conservative party that opposed this policy, maybe Nick Clegg did a deal, maybe he had to back down. Humiliating for him and horrifying for the electorate who believed him, but was it a sacrifice he had to make to work as a coalition to achieve other important goals. This feels like *Facebook* could have been in a similar situation with the restrictive and draconian government policies on Covid. Did they want to do and say more, but were unable to? I know many reading this would be horrified that I am in anyway making excuses for *Facebook*. But I do look back now and feel there is a possibility that they tried their best. And I was banned from my *Facebook* channels on at least six occasions and at one point was unable to do my training through an important group I have on there. It was humiliating and embarrassing to lose *Facebook*. I am just trying to ask important questions about how we need to work with opposing sides.

What I do know is that the important journalism I did in 2020 is still on *Facebook*. They allowed me to broadcast vitally important interviews with protestors in central London, while other long established media brands were calling them conspiracy nuts. Being there and speaking to these people, it was very clear they were not.

One particular broadcast from the 27th September 2020, has 471k views on *Facebook*. It had the same number of views on my *YouTube* channel but a week or two later they took it down. I am now demonetised on *YouTube* just because of that video. So really compared to *Facebook* have been good to me in comparison.

I feel *Twitter* should also get a mention here, as again they allowed me to publish all of the interviews and footage from the London protests.

I can tell you now, I would not have fancied the job as Comms Directory for any of these companies in 2020 and 2021. Very difficult decisions had to be made, and we need to recognise and appreciate that.

CHAPTER TEN - Moving on

I have seen first-hand how parents are vaccinating their children based on the media brand they trust and that may be *Facebook*, *YouTube*, the *BBC* or the *Guardian*, or the influencer they follow on *Bitchute*, *Brand New Tube*, or *Telegram*. There appears to be no middle ground. No 50:50 debate and my goodness me how much do I care about that; how much do I want to fight for that?

Social media, however, was able to allow us to hear other voices. Alternative media we call it, provided the alternative view.

But we need to recognise that there are many media organisations which are simply a person, I would not say they are profit or ego motivated, but they don't understand how debate brings unity. They don't have journalistic qualifications, so don't understand how valuable it is to get a right of reply, find a regulator and put in place a complaints procedure. There is no balance, just one view. It has been hugely damaging for the citizen journalism movement.

These are passionate caring and brave people, but they keep pumping out a one-sided view in terms of the medical professionals they trust. But it is shouting into that echo chamber, saying the same things to the same people. And not reaching a confused audience, but like I said could be feeding an ignorant audience, or a deeply cynical one, with no in-between.

Because of censorship people have had to rely on the anecdotal stories around them; Dave down the road who at 52 had a heart condition and died unvaccinated with Covid. Their auntie's best mate, who at 31, unvaccinated, died in hospital from Covid after giving birth to a healthy baby. Their mother-in-law who had a stroke after her booster, their cousin's plumber who left three children and died suddenly in his sleep aged just 45.

These are the stories I hear. And I will now share with you three messages sent within a few days from professional contacts I know in a WhatsApp group. I won't share any more details about their profession as I do not want to reveal who they are. But they come from senior positions in business, public protection, education and health. Some retired some still working.

I had said in a tweet that I felt the GB News Mark Steyn broadcast on the 13th July 2022 where he spoke to the families and individuals who had experienced vaccine injury or death was not balanced.

After that, I lost a lot of friends and supporters. It was very upsetting for me. One close friend I haven't heard from since.

But to sum up some of the other responses and the conversation that followed, these are three messages I had from professional contacts.

Hi all, I've come to the decision that I'm going to have to leave this group, I respect you all but I cannot stay on any group where people feel that these poison / death / injury jabs are any good for anyone at any age.

I've directly known of three people who have been killed due to the jabs and have numerous friends and family seriously injured by them.

I've only just found out that another friend's daughter is in critical care (since Monday) and she's only in her twenties after a seizure that they cannot work out what caused it, she's hanging on, she has no previous health conditions whatsoever and this now is sadly common practice.

Her family know my stance and her mother said when informing me (instantly), she had her 3rd jab months ago so it can't be that, what do I say, I don't say anything on this occasion as I am silenced by virtue of what the media has done to society.

Traditional media are total scum in my opinion and they continue to peddle the agenda of the World Economic Forum (WEF) / World Health Organisation/WHO and we know who are controlling them as they are controlling 90% of the media and those who know and willingly go along or turn a blind eye within the media will have their day of reckoning.

You could see the glee on the faces of traditional media when people were being threatened with no jab no job, they have lost all respect and will never get it back again because they are not journalists but bought pawns by the globalist elites.

I have contact details with a few of the group who I will most definitely stay in contact with as I have the upmost respect for who stood up when we were the few, all warriors in my book.

Thank you for those who took time to share material which is evidence enough of the true evil at work here and the damage that the jabs are doing.

I don't dislike those who have had the jabs as many believed it was either, the right thing to do or for the greater good and willingly gave their trust due to what they were being told 24/7 on the radio, press and TV, even now the facts are totally suppressed, only 50% of those who have been double jabbed have had the booster and the latest figures of hospitalisations and deaths from 'Covid' are 90% of those who have had three or four jabs (go figure) yet our media stay silent on these FACTS.

I wish you and your families good health and all the best for the future, love and respect.

And another message here on the group:

Thought I'd add my ten-pennorth on this lively discussion about balance in the media...

Since the start of Covid the media have failed to provide any balance in their output. For two and a half years we have only seen one side of the argument on mainstream media. Therefore, in my mind balance can only be provided by a competing team giving the other side. Think of it like two football teams competing in the FA Cup, say Liverpool and Accrington Stanley, you wouldn't expect the Liverpool team to consist of all Liverpool players and the Accrington Stanley team to be half Accrington players and half Liverpool players. That's where we're now at with Covid. Because it has become so polarised in one direction; that of the dominant team. In order to address the lack of balance we need a competing team that doesn't also help the already dominant team, which has a massive advantage. For me that's the nub of the problem. Balance in a programme is not providing balance at all, it's merely further kneecapping the lower division team needlessly.

I recognise we all have opinions which differ but there's not one of you in this group who I wouldn't want standing by me going into battle. As Anna says it's all about trust and you all have mine and I trust that we can disagree but also remain a team (family even) looking out for each other xx

And another:

Can anyone help with some guidance please?

This morning at our weekly SITP a man who presents as very sensible, was calmly telling me that the vaxxed show up on a Bluetooth app on a smartphone. This he said, is because the jab has implanted nano chips that each have a Bluetooth code. I've heard this before and thought it had been rejected as false, but he was assuring me it is true!

Three exceptionally interesting messages really sums up the mess that we are in. One person in the WhatsApp group commented on that last message re Bluetooth and the vaxxed was total nonsense, but it was not delivered in a kind and gentle way.

I have left many WhatsApp groups because I can't stand it. I know many people feel the same, they just leave when they can't engage with what they deem to be nonsense. They find it disturbing to have once been in a group of sane, sensible people to find themselves among peers asking weird and embarrassing questions. But I have met these sane professional people asking these weird and embarrassing questions.

A woman who got in touch with me via *Twitter*, who was once an MSM newspaper reporter, called me on my landline telephone and said after vaccination that she had become magnetic and cutlery was sticking to her. She begged me for an hour of my time, saying she needed help, clarity and someone to bring her back to normality and sanity. I said "I can't help you and I won't take your money. I said you need to reach deep into your heart, mind and soul and feel what is right and what is true. I am not here to be your guide on these matters."

But over the last two years I have seen something that I am happy to comment on. That shame is a bigger motivator than fear of death. There are parents I know who have children with asthma and they were too ashamed to ask for mask exemption for their children while at school. Not wanting to be seen as a "granny killer". Or whatever dominant narrative there was at the time from MSM or their peers in terms of mask wearing and the risk Covid posed.

It was horrific to witness how gutless people became when their own children were suffering. I have found it fascinating to observe over the last 900 days how shame seems to drive so many. Putting it before the health and safety of their own children.

It has made me feel detached from the general population. I know I am not alone here; many have experienced similar. Close family and friends behaving in a way that we could never have comprehended as possible. People we admired and respected, wired by fear, illogical fear and unable and unwilling to listen to an alternative narrative.

We have all been asking ourselves:

"How do I look? How do I look if I meet a very credible person who asks a question that seems ridiculous, do I even have the courage to engage in conversation? Or do I simply ignore and move away?"

The problem we now face in 2022 is that we don't know what nonsense is anymore. Could that many doctors be wrong is an important question.

I have really struggled to write this book; it has been immensely difficult - emotionally draining.

I can't move on until we all move on and recognise the mistakes we made, that we can never make again.

People I liked and respected behaved in a way that I don't recognise, their behaviour and actions were illogical. So to belong to a society that makes sense, to connect with a community that I can understand and respect is what will keep me going. I know I am not alone.

This book needs to be written. It needs to be talked about. We need to never allow this to happen again, but we also need to move on.

These WhatsApp messages show the damage that has been done. But we must try hard to find a way out of this. Old media, old government - the old way of doing things must be replaced by a new and exciting future.

I saw brave, wonderful people that I adored for their courage and compassion going to GB News, but for me that isn't the answer either.

I shared a recent post on my Patreon about GB News which I think is important. The title is, "I am asking you to do something that I could not do."

This is what it said.

"Activism is an interesting word, for me it means you are so passionate about something it just bursts through in everything you say and do. It is congruent, it is real, but does it

put people off if they don't feel the same way?

Journalism is trying your very best to hide how you truly feel and let the public listen to the arguments and make up their own mind. The odd thing now with social media is that we really don't need this bridge between content and the public. And that is a huge challenge for the future of journalism which I don't think really even exists any more. There is content and there is trust.

An interesting chat I had with a former colleague who is now at Sky News. He called me an activist and said that is not an insult – he said you are a good campaigner, but you are not a journalist. I really remember this and took it on board and thought yes maybe he is right. When it came to seeing children suffer during Covid it was very hard to not let this burst through in everything I did.

So I did a video yesterday explaining why I felt Dan Wootton describing the GB News audience as a community/family concerned me.

How GB News feels a bit like we are breathing a sigh of relief and finally feel validated – but is that news and is it going to reach everyone? We must think about the purpose of what we are publishing and the intended consequences of that, so I often put myself in my sister's shoes and I find that really helps. I want her to rely on a media organisation that provides the arguments for and against vaccination before she makes an important decision for herself and her children.

I told her the other day, I have been asked on GB News and she said, "What is GB News?"

I then asked her "Do you watch the news?"

She said, "No we don't have time with the three young children but we keep up to date on the BBC News app."

If you look at BARB (the industry guide for linear/ terrestrial TV viewing figures) the top 30 programmes, the BBC News at six is the highest performing news programme, getting around five to six million at its absolute peak, on a Monday or Tuesday and when the weather isn't great. ITV National news on their best night can get around 2.5 million but never any more than that.

GB News, according to Dan Wootton, has been close to the viewing figures for the news channels BBC and Sky and even beating them lately. This is low approx. around 100k. When you look at the UK population of 67 million this really puts it into perspective. Most people are watching something funny or entertaining, I am sure.

But when it comes to the news I don't care if we are talking about lockdown, or masks or vaccines, or climate change, or monkeypox. Or if there is some strange disease people are linking to our tap water. It really honestly does not matter what the topic is, what matters is we have somewhere to go to listen to BOTH sides, that is balanced and to put our faith and trust in that. Not activism and campaigning which is what I am guilty of.

Taking yourself out of journalism is exceptionally difficult and when you are touched emotionally and hear someone's pain, you often sway to their side. Then you forget about the other side. It is the hardest thing to stay out of your content, that is something I learnt when training to be a counsellor. It is the same thing, your "own stuff" needs to come out of the counselling relationship with a client.

So is GB News getting it wrong? Only as much as I did. But it feels like the views of influencers with big Twitter accounts has been turned into a TV News programme. It is opinion during the hour, then news on the hour. How can these two comfortably sit together? It is better to be honest and call it GB Opinions not GB News.

I also know that seeing a grinning Nigel Farage as a headline presenter would put my sister off. Simply because he has in the past stated his political position. Like I said it is very hard to go from campaigner to journalist. You can go from journalist to campaigner but then it's very hard to go back. In fact, I think it is impossible because you have shown what you care about, your passion, your values and your opinions. So then to try and put across a balanced view is really tough, people deep down will know what you really think.

I am asking GB News to do what I can't. I have been vocal in providing a one-sided counter narrative and for that I am very proud. I had to act quickly as a one-woman band, doing Zoom interviews on my laptop during the crisis. Like a retired doctor rushing back to help the NHS, I felt like a journalist coming out of my training career back into journalism, because there was an emergency.

What I keep thinking though is what I could do with the funding and the team at GB News and I would be going in a very different direction. I would be trying to get my sister to replace that BBC news app with a GB News one.

I know someone like Dan Wootton, for example, has a large team of producers working with him. That would be a dream for me. A one-man band with a mobile or a laptop is probably going to struggle more to provide a balanced and impartial news channel.

So if I were at GB News, I would attach a newsroom, where we would teach members of the public how to make the most of their mobiles and social media platforms, to get out a truth we are not hearing. Then taking *some of the best of that content and putting it on the channel.*

And if I were doing a piece on vaccination I would make sure the debate was 50:50 with experts of similar calibre head-to-head. That is tough though, I do appreciate that.

My sister is not part of the GB News family or community. She trusts the BBC and wanted Hilary Clinton to be the first ever female US president in 2016.

I am getting a lot of criticism for airing these views. Wouldn't it be easier for me to just be a part of the GB News family and go on as a pundit as many other influencers have who, like me, fought lockdown?

I could promote my courses and my books and not get any abuse. Not be called a shill, not be told I am constantly flip flopping. Wouldn't my life be happier, easier and I would make money and be respected by THAT community.

But I am not in a community, I don't need validation. I need a news service that we can all trust, one that I know my sister can go to. One that in the future my children can go to.

It is chaos out there. And it scares the life out of me.

I see presenters like Mark Steyn, Dan Wootton, Bev Turner, Neil Oliver doing some really important interviews and raising awareness when other media brands have simply smeared and shamed. But I know I couldn't take my feelings out of it and if I tried to people would know. They could see on my face that I was pretending.

What I can say is that I know an ICU doctor who had to tell a husband his 31-year-old wife who had just given birth had died. She had Covid and was unvaccinated. He said most of the Covid deaths were unvaccinated back in 2021, he was anti lockdown and I trust him. So, I listened to this.

I met a senior nurse on holiday in Crete this year and she described to me what life was like on a Covid ward in the spring of 2020. How she had to rush from one dying patient to the other with an iPad so they could say goodbye to their loved ones. She said they had to leave people to die, they couldn't treat them all and had to make unbearable decisions about who to save. She still had a look of shock and horror in her eyes as the told me this, she said many of her colleagues had horrific PTSD and had to leave the NHS.

I don't think it is straightforward and I am struggling to find voices and news channels I trust. Could it be that the vaccine has saved lives and killed people? Could it be that lockdown saved some and killed others?

And finally, I think about Charlotte Wright who lost her husband Dr Stephen Wright following complications with the AZ vaccine. I think about that family and how they trusted the information they heard about the vaccine coming from the Government and media brands such as Sky and the BBC. So, I ask myself, would they have watched GB News? This is really important, as another crisis will undoubtedly come along. I think, like my sister, the grinning Nigel Farage would probably mean they wouldn't necessarily see GB News as an impartial news channel and would not then potentially listen to important information on whether or not the vaccine was right for them.

As I said, each day when we wake up and post on social media or communicate on WhatsApp, what are we trying to achieve? I want a safe and happy future for my children and all children where they can thrive and when a public health emergency or any other emergency comes along they can really trust the Government and a media organisation to hold that Government to account. And to provide ALL the information they need to make up their own minds.

News channels are not there to make us feel validated, to make us feel better. They are there to challenge us and to open our minds to all views. Each day we must be willing to listen, we must never stop listening and stop caring about society as a whole and how we can all work together for the best possible future for our children. Being rigid, listening to the same content and opinions over and over again within our echo chambers is incredibly dangerous."

That was the post I published to Patreon and some people understood this but many did not.

The last interview I did with a doctor was Dr Chris Milburn and I was totally worn out. Like a soldier with PTSD, I knew deep down I could not do this any more. He was Head of Emergency medicine in Nova Scotia in Canada and had spoken out on the equivalent of the local BBC questioning the government narrative on Covid and lost his job. For me this was the straw that broke the camel's back. I couldn't take it any more. I had seen too many brave people fall. Too much pain, too much suffering with no reward.

He lost his job for caring. How many people did I speak to who lost their job? Too many. That is all they were trying to do, help us.

And I couldn't cope with any more pain from brave people. I wanted to see action from those who were hiding. Those who knew it was wrong and did nothing.

Only seeing that would give me the impetus to fight on, with optimism. I have to give these people the skills to take it on, to mobilise those around them. To publish in a way that does get everyone listening, that unites us to fight for a future we are really excited about. To not constantly keep publishing to the same people with the same message. But to bring us all together.

We cannot allow this to ever happen again and these old institutions will fail us again. Whatever you want to call it, the established, legacy, dinosaur media. We will not tolerate it. We will get back the power – we have new media. And we have a chance to change our future.

The future belongs to those people we all remember who have a huge following on social media thanks to their bravery and courage.

As I come to the end of the book, I do worry that paranoia and cynicism has set in, rigid and unrelenting for many. I see a lack of hope when I watch and read some new media content.

It feels like people believe the protests and all that suffering was for nothing. Well I saw it working. When travelling to Paris for a holiday this year, my host told me that all health workers in France were forced to have the vaccine or lose their jobs. That did not happen here.

Again with vaccine passports, we saw them introduced almost everywhere in Europe. That did not happen in the same way here. I needed a vaccine passport to go to the cinema in Wales for a month or two, but that was the only impact I experienced. I once interviewed Tania O'Sullivan living in Lithuania who had to ask others to buy her baby milk. Those interviews and others are still on the website againstvaccinepassports.com

We had the Together Declaration, UsForThem, Against Vaccine Passports, NHS100k, Save Our Rights UK, A Stand in the Park, and so many more groups, did their fight mean nothing, did we not make a difference?

You need to get noticed by those in power, i.e. put forward a credible argument that those in power will listen to and one that challenges them. Or put yourself forward to be elected, so you have the power to make the changes you want to see.

We can do that with new media - filming, and publishing with our mobiles. But too much content seems to be a massive whinge or anxiety fest. I don't see people believing they can make a difference. I see them scared, and writing articles and forming new groups when there are already so many organisations and campaign groups out there.

Lots of panic. Sometimes I feel people have given up thinking they can make a difference. They are waiting, and I guess I am also waiting for that big party.

Will I get that day where my children smile at me, and say Mum we are so proud of you. Your work did make a difference.

I finish the book in October 2022, and I don't feel we are moving in the right direction. We are acting like the underdog; our media content is poor. We call them the mainstream and we are not acting like the mainstream.

We allow people to share and discuss everything as if it might be true, without any challenge.

Trust is in short supply everywhere, and we need to ask ourselves how we can build that up again - and fast.

We do need to really truly believe that we do have a say in our future, our communication as journalists, because that is what we all are now - journalists. But our content needs to be better if we are going to turn this around.

We need to beat the journalists at their own game and produce balanced, calm, thought provoking content, that builds trust and brings us all together.

This book is the end of Covid for me, I am looking forward to the future where I help you all to film, edit and publish at speed professional content that puts the old media to shame. I know you can do it.

Printed in Great Britain
by Amazon